100 Questions and Answers About Gen X

Forged by economics, technology, pop culture and work

Michigan State University
School of Journalism

Front Edge Publishing

For more information and further discussion, visit
news.jrn.msu.edu/culturalcompetence/

Cover art and design by
Rick Nease
www.RickNeaseArt.com

Published by
Front Edge Publishing, LLC
42015 Ford Road, Suite 234
Canton, Michigan

Front Edge Publishing specializes in speed and flexibility
in adapting and updating our books. We can include
links to video and other online media. We offer discounts
on bulk purchases for special events, corporate training,
and small groups. We are able to customize bulk orders
by adding corporate or event logos on the cover and
we can include additional pages inside describing your
event or corporation. For more information about our
fast and flexible publishing or permission to use our
materials, please contact Front Edge Publishing at info@
FrontEdgePublishing.com.

Contents

Acknowledgments

The authors of this book are: (front row, from left) Camille Douglas, Marisa Ruggirello, Kelsi A. Horn, Kenedi Robinson, Sondos Hosam Gharib; (middle row, from left) Paige Boyd, Lauren Shields, Hauwa Abbas, Heather Maxon, John Lavaccare, Jingjing Nie; (third row, from left) Jalen J. Smith, Daniel Rayzel, Alexandra Donlin, Eve Kucharski and Katie Dudlets. Not shown: Emalie Parsons.

The class, a bunch of Gen Z people led by a Boomer, needed a lot of help. We had some excellent advisers.

Tim Smith, visionary owner of Skidmore Studio, graciously drove from Detroit to our classroom in East Lansing to talk about generations. Skidmore crafts "brand strategy, design and messaging for companies in the business of food and fun." Smith had recently published "Dare Mighty Things: A Field Guide for Millennial Entrepreneurs." Smith died in 2018 at age 54 and was remembered by the studio as, "Never one to accept the way things have been done, Tim was always focused on what's next." We are honored that this guide is a small part of that.

Cynthia Wang is features editor at TV Week in Sydney. She has been a senior writer and content editor at Who Magazine, the Australian sister publication to People and Entertainment Weekly. She was a writer, editor and reporter at People Magazine for 18 years. She earned her bachelor's degree from Northwestern's Medill School of Journalism in 1993. Wang remembers the day she came home from school and saw that the family TV was connected to cable. Her father called to tell her not to turn it on until he got home. Too late. The first thing she saw on MTV was a J. Geils Band video. Wang is smack-dab in the middle of Generation X and proud of it.

Richard Epps is web and publication design professor in the Michigan State University School of Journalism, from which he graduated in 1993. Epps had a 20-year career at The Detroit News as presentation editor, news design director, sports designer and front-page designer. Epps previously worked at The Record in Troy, New York, and at The News-Herald, in Mentor, Ohio.

Professor and MSU School of Journalism Director **Lucinda Davenport** has supported this series with enthusiasm, as she does most things.

Introduction

By Cynthia Wang

If there is a generation with a chip on its shoulder, this is it. Gen Xers have our reasons.

Smaller than the generations that bookend it, Gen X is not a demographic darling. Gen Xers feel ignored, unnoticed, under-appreciated and overlooked by politicians, marketers and researchers. That's OK with us. We are used to fending for ourselves.

Sandwiched between Boomers born to Ozzie and Harriet parents and everyone-gets-a-trophy Millennials, Gen Xers often had to let ourselves in after school because Mom and Dad were at work.

We were children of the Cold War between the United States and the Soviet Union. We kept one eye on the Doomsday Clock, worried about nuclear destruction, and the other eye on MTV. But seeing the Berlin Wall fall made us think we really were giving peace a chance. That, and seeing a solitary man stand in front of a tank in Beijing's Tiananmen Square, made most Gen Xers, regardless of politics, doubt the effectiveness of walls.

We watched the Space Shuttle Challenger, with civilian teacher Christa McAuliffe on board, explode on live TV, and we saw Prince Charles and Princess Diana get married on TV, too.

Live Aid in 1985 and subsequent all-star concerts melded the ideals of Woodstock with the activism of our generation. The concerts raised money to fight hunger in Africa and AIDS, to help farmers, and to heal the world. The idea was that to effect change you have to work outside the government. That, rather than politics, became this generation's path.

The activism of a generation raised on MTV was channeled through music and pop culture. Gen X remembers Al Gore not for being the "Inconvenient Truth" guy, but for being the husband of Tipper Gore, who Xers saw as fighting freedom of speech with her Parents Music Resource Center, which sought to label explicit content in music. That led to the spectacle of Frank Zappa and Dee Snider from Twisted Sister testifying before Congress and put Gen X forever on the side of laissez-faire labeling, even if we do use those guides now as parents. Things happen to Gen X, and we carry on.

Gen X saw the Sept. 11, 2001, terror attacks, the L.A. riots, the O.J. Simpson trial, and the Waco, Texas, siege. We also saw the cultural and political tide turn in the rise of the African American, Asian American, Latinx and LGBTQ American collective identity.

After the 1990s tech boom, Gen Xers who had become entrepreneurs were caught in the dot-com bust of 1999-2001. As they got on their feet and as younger Gen Xers were starting their careers, Gen X ran into the housing collapse and the Great Recession of 2007-2009, the worst in 80 years. Now, Gen Xers must care (and pay) for our parents and our children while our own retirement seems further in the distance.

While other generations largely dislike the labels others have imposed, some members of this generation embrace the X.

Rebellious Gen Xers tore up public stairways and concrete with skateboard tricks, creating the X Games. Later, Millennials' parents made things safer with sanctioned skate parks.

Gen X has become the political watershed between younger generations and the right-leaning Baby Boom and Greatest Generations. Now ascending in power as Boomers retire, Gen Xers, a smaller age cohort, must be the bridge that links the generations.

Preface

Change is cascading through the generations, triggering turning points in the United States and the world.

In 2015, the number of Millennials in U.S. workplaces bypassed Baby Boomers, who are turning 65 at the rate of 10,000 each day. Millennials had already passed Generation X, which enjoyed just three years as the largest working generation, sandwiched as it is between two larger cohorts.

Then, in the heat of the 2016 presidential campaign, the Census Bureau reported that Millennials had surpassed Boomers as the country's largest living generation, on the brink of becoming the largest generation of voters. That April, there were 69.2 million voting-age Millennials, compared to 69.7 million Boomers. The United States has now had four Boomer presidents: George W. Bush, Bill Clinton, Barack Obama and Donald Trump. As the third president born in 1946, the first year of the Baby Boom, Trump became the oldest president ever elected. His election gave Boomers at least a 28-year lock on the White House.

Major pivots are on the horizon. Using United Nations data, Bloomberg predicts that Gen Z will overtake Millennials as the largest generation on the planet in 2019.

As workforce leaders, Gen Xers will have to connect Boomers and Millennials. That will be complicated by the arrivals of post-Millennials. Some call this the first time in U.S. history that four generations have had to work together.

There is disagreement on when generations begin and end, which contributes to variance in how large each generation is. We use years designated by the Pew Research Center, whose work has provided invaluable help in this series. Even reliable Pew changed its Millennial/Gen Z turning point in 2018. These are the birth years Pew now uses for each generation:

Before 1928	Greatest
1928-1945	Silent
1946-1964	Baby Boomer
1965-1980	Gen X
1981-1996	Millennial
1997-	Gen Z
	(subject to change)

The Gen X section of this double guide pays significant attention to changes in technology and pop culture.

Joe Grimm
Series editor
School of Journalism
Michigan State University

Demographics

1 When was Gen X born?

Generations do not have crisp cutoffs, and different researchers use different years. Generally, people born from the mid 1960s to the late 1970s or early 1980s are called Generation X. In this guide, we are using 1965-1980 from the Pew Research Center.

2 How many Gen Xers are there?

This is a smaller generation than the ones that came before and after. There were an estimated 66 million Gen Xers in the United States in 2015. Gen X enjoyed just three years as the largest U.S. generation in the workforce, from 2012 to 2015. Then, the Millennials overtook them.

3 Where did Generation X get its name?

Some attribute the name to "Class X," a chapter in the 1983 book, "Class: A Guide Through the American Status System," by Paul Fussell. In 1991, demographers William Strauss and Neil Howe published their groundbreaking study "Generations:

The History of America's Future, 1584 to 2069."
They labeled the post-Boomer group as the 13th
Generation. They continued to in 1993 with the
publication of, "13th Gen: Abort, Retry, Ignore, Fail?"
Douglas Coupland's 1991 novel, "Generation X:
Tales for an Accelerated Culture," helped popularize
the tag. In later editions, Strauss and Howe's
"Generations" includes the term Gen X.

4 Why is Gen X smaller than other generations?

There is no set length for generations, and Gen
X had fewer birth years than the previous three.
Additionally, the birth rate was lower during the Gen
X birth years.

5 Is this why Gen X is called the Forgotten Generation?

Yes. The Baby Boomer (77 million) and Millennial
(83 million) generations surround Gen X, sometimes
causing people to skip the "forgotten middle
child." Marketers overlooked Gen X, according to
AdWeek, jumping from Boomers to Millennials.
In 2019, the online news network CBSN posted a
graphic about generations and left out Gen X. One
person tweeted, "Er, you forgot one, @CBSNLive.
#GenX? You may remember us as the inventors
of Harry Potter, podcasting and irony." Many Gen
Xers say "just forget it." According to a study by
MetLife insurance company, only 41 percent of this

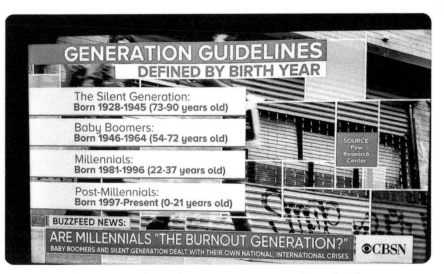

GENERATION GUIDELINES
DEFINED BY BIRTH YEAR

The Silent Generation:
Born 1928-1945 (73-90 years old)

Baby Boomers:
Born 1946-1964 (54-72 years old)

Millennials:
Born 1981-1996 (22-37 years old)

Post-Millennials:
Born 1997-Present (0-21 years old)

SOURCE:
Pew
Research
Center

BUZZFEED NEWS:

ARE MILLENNIALS "THE BURNOUT GENERATION?"
BABY BOOMERS AND SILENT GENERATION DEALT WITH THEIR OWN NATIONAL, INTERNATIONAL CRISES ⊙CBSN

generation identifies as Gen Xers. It has also been called the Lost Generation, lost between two bigger ones. Other names include the MTV Generation and the Latchkey Generation, for children who came from school to empty homes because of the rise of two-income families.

6 Why have Gen Xers been called "slackers?"

The stereotype implies disinterest and lack of direction. The label was enshrined with the 1991 Richard Linklater film "Slacker," when many Gen Xers were young. The movie was about under-30 adults in Austin, Texas. Alternatively, National Geographic attributed the label to the Oct. 19, 1987, stock market swoon. That day, the Dow Jones Industrial Average fell 22.6 percent. It was the largest one-day fall in history, even larger than the one that started the Great Depression. It disrupted traditional occupations and career paths just as Gen X was hitting the job market. Today, perhaps because of how that changed job prospects, some Gen Xers are seen not as slackers but as workaholic entrepreneurs.

7 What is the racial makeup of Gen X in the United States?

Each generation has been more diverse than the one that preceded it. In the 2040s, it is expected that so-called minorities will be most of the U.S. population. Gen X has shown the greatest change in that direction so far. The percentage of non-Hispanic Whites declined from 73 percent of Baby Boomers to 62 percent for Gen Xers. According to a Pew analysis, Gen X is 18 percent Hispanic, 12 percent non-Hispanic Black, 6 percent non-Hispanic Asian and 2 percent other.

8 How confident are Gen Xers about their futures?

Confidence seems to slip a little with each generation. In a 2017 Country Financial study, 27 percent of Baby Boomers said they expected to be worse off. That compared to 31 percent of Gen Xers and 40 percent of Millennials. Carol Hymowitz wrote in Bloomberg News in 2015, "Gen Xers are still paying off student loans while raising families on wages that have barely budged in recent years. They have more debt than other age groups and are more pessimistic about ever being able to afford to retire ..."

9 What makes Gen Xers alike?

While individuals within every generation are different, shared experiences sweep over them. Recognizing that one generation spans 16-20 years, even incidents that affect many do so in different ways. Age and perspective are powerful filters. So, we'll spend more time with key events and examinations of how Generation X thinks and acts overall than we will with labels. Some of their greatest shared experiences are in the next section. Their responses to those events follow.

10 How do Gen Xers describe themselves?

They disagree. The terms they mentioned most frequently in a MetLife study were opposites and were not mentioned by even 10 percent of respondents. Eight percent said their generation is hard-working. Five percent said it is lazy. In 2010, Pew Research asked adults of all ages if their generation was unique. About 60 percent of Baby Boomers and Millennials said yes. Only half of Gen Xers said so. Twenty-eight percent of Gen Xers said they related more with Boomers. Twelve percent said they related to Millennials.

11 What are differences between early and late Gen Xers?

The gap between the beginning and end of Gen X made for distinct differences in experiences and values. People born near the edges of generations are called cuspers. They can be like the generation nearest to their own. Some Gen Xers born just after the Baby Boom reflect its generally more conservative values. The youngest Gen Xers may vote more like Millennials. For example, Pew found that only 32 percent of Boomers wanted bigger government, while 53 percent of Millennials preferred more services. Pew found that mid-spectrum Gen Xers were closer to their generation's average on politics and technology.

12 Who are Xennials?

Late Gen X and early Millennial cuspers share some experiences. Writer Sarah Stankorb described Xennials in Good magazine as occupying "a fleeting sweet spot before the Recession that plagued Millennials' launch. Yet we were still young enough that when the market crashed, we hadn't yet invested much and didn't lose as many homes or as much in retirement savings, unlike many Gen Xers. We at least had a chance to either get jobs or go to college as young adults, then attain more serious jobs, quit them, get other jobs, and find ourselves just a little before the economy truly tanked ... Our micro-generation attended much of secondary school in a pre-Columbine era. September 11 was formative for us." Some label this cohort, born between 1977 and 1985, as the Oregon Trail Generation after an early video game. They experienced analog and digital, cynicism and optimism and some wicked economic times.

Seismic Events

13 How have recessions affected Generation X?

Gen X has experienced economic turbulence at vulnerable times. After the boom years of the 1990s, when they were young adults, they were slammed by the burst of the dot-com bubble in 1999-2001. Many Gen X tech entrepreneurs were caught in that crash. As they were recovering in their 30s and 40s, the Great Recession hit them.

14 How did 9/11 affect Gen X?

When the Twin Towers were attacked on Sept. 11, 2001, Gen Xers were 21 and older with adult understanding of political events. Many Gen Xers participated in the U.S. invasion of Iraq two years later.

15 What effect did the Columbine shootings have?

The 1999 school killings came just after the last Gen Xers had finished high school. The attack forever changed the thinking and dialogue about a host of issues. They included school safety, childhood innocence, mental health and gun laws. That tragedy and others that followed made Gen X the first one to raise its children with a new set of worries.

16 How has immigration affected this generation?

As Generation X began in the mid 1960s, U.S. immigration law changed drastically. The Immigration and Naturalization Act of 1965 abolished a 40-year-old quota system based on national origin. The new policy was based on reuniting families and attracting skilled labor. In the 30 years after passage of the law, more than 18 million immigrants legally entered the United States. That was triple the number admitted over the preceding 30 years. For the first time in generations, larger numbers immigrated from Asia, Africa and other places. Gen Xers from around the world continue to immigrate to the United States. The median age of immigrants coming to the United States in 2013, according to the Migration Policy Institute, was 43.1. They are members of this generation.

17 How did HIV/AIDS affect Generation X?

The federal website HIV.gov started its HIV/AIDS timeline in 1981, just after the last Gen Xer was born. This means the disease went undetected and untreated in older Gen Xers. According to the U.S. Centers for Disease Control and Prevention, 42 percent of people diagnosed with HIV in 2013 were 50 and older. Thirty-nine percent of 6,721 HIV deaths in 2014 were people 55 and older. Gen X remembers the AIDS-related death of actor Rock Hudson in 1985. The death of teenager Ryan White from AIDS complications in 1990 made many covers of People and became a television movie. NBA player Magic Johnson came out with his HIV diagnosis in 1991. AIDS played a major role in Jonathan Larson's 1994 musical "Rent."

Values

18 What are top Gen X values?

Gen Xers' values reflect their middle-child label. According to a 2017 Pew Research study, Gen Xers fall between Millennials and Boomers on value questions. Sixty-five percent of Gen Xers agreed that same-sex marriage should be legal. Sixty-two percent said the country should do more to ensure that Blacks have the same rights as Whites. Sixty-six percent said immigration strengthens the country. Twenty-six percent said the U.S. border with Mexico should be substantially expanded.

19 What religions do Gen Xers practice?

According to a 2014 Pew survey of Gen Xers, the largest group, 25 percent, said they were evangelical Christians. Next were people who said they were not affiliated with a religion, at 23 percent. Then came Catholics, 21 percent, and mainline Protestants, at 13 percent. Non-Christian religions were 6 percent.

20 Is Gen X less religious than previous generations?

In terms of organized religion, yes. They reflect a rising trend across the United States and around the world. Seventeen percent of Baby Boomers and 35 percent of Millennials said they were religiously unaffiliated, while 23 percent of Gen Xers said so. This was in the Pew Religious Landscape report issued in 2015.

Generation X Religious Landscape

Pew Research Center 2015 Religious Landscape Study. "Other Christian Groups" included Mormons, Orthodox Christians, Jehovah's Witnesses and other smaller Christian groups.

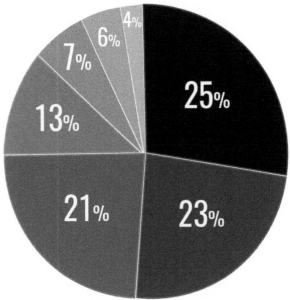

- Evangelical Protestant (25%)
- Unaffiliated (23%)
- Catholic (21%)
- Mainline Protestant (13%)
- Historically Black Protestant (7%)
- Other Groups (6%)
- Other Christian Groups (4%)

Technology

21 How did technology change for Gen X?

So many ways: affordable digital watches, calculators, push-button phones, microwave ovens. Beepers to pagers to mobile phones to smartphones. AM to FM to digital. Photography went from film to digital and then into phones. Computer technology transformed from Gen Xers' childhood days in the 1970s and '80s into adulthood. The 1990s saw the advent of the internet, the rise of cellphones and laptop computers, Palm Pilots and BlackBerrys. The 2000s saw the rise of text messaging, Wi-Fi, and smartphones. The 2010s gave rise to tablets, wearable technology and smart home technology. Music went from vinyl 45s and albums to 8-track tapes to cassettes to CDs to downloading and streaming. The Sony Walkman gave way to the Discman and eventually the iPod, which led to smartphones. In television, the game-changers were widespread cable TV, the VCR, then DVD, Blu-Ray, then PVR and streaming services. In computing, the typewriter went electric, then went to microprocessing, basic computers, and then the PC and Apple revolution in personal computing. The latter benefitted from the growth of Wi-Fi. Gamers saw Atari, Coleco and Intellivision come out with in-home devices in the late '70s and early '80s. Videographers went from film through iterations of digital cameras and camcorders to cameras in phones.

22 How did technology change video watching?

This generation witnessed the rise and demise of home video rentals. VCRs were introduced to the public in 1977. Their cost fell from $1,200 to $50 as people bought millions of them. Blockbuster opened its first video rental store in 1985 and started to decline after Netflix came in 1997. The DVD market started in 1999, also with $1,200 players. Gas stations, grocery stores and motels had movie rental counters or shelves. TiVo introduced digital video recording in 1999, making it possible for Gen Xers, who by then were all adults, to record TV shows, watch them whenever they wanted and skip the commercials. Cable TV had been around since the 1940s, but was shackled by finances and regulations until the 1970s. Cable subscribers quadrupled from 10 million in 1975 to 40 million in 1985. Cable networks almost tripled from 28 in 1980 to 79 in 1990.

23 How did technology affect Gen Xers as young adults?

Many Gen Xers work every day with technology that did not exist when they were in school. They are the last generation not to be considered digital natives because they grew up in the 1970s and '80s before wireless communication. A 2016 Payscale study showed Silicon Valley has age-stratified workplaces. It found that tech employees were much younger than the average U.S. age of 42. These were average ages at some tech giants: Microsoft, 33; Apple, 31; Amazon 30; and Facebook 29. All are in Millennial territory.

24 Are Gen Xers good at technology?

They excel at it. Although Millennials are called "digital natives," Gen Xers were early adopters who quickly adapted to computer gaming and work. Gen Xers express as much confidence as Millennials in their use of technology. Gen X also uses social media more than any other generation, according to a 2016 Nielsen report.

25 How else did phones change for Gen X?

For one thing, there was a lot more talking on landlines—some with cords. According to Census Bureau data, as of 1998, when Gen Xers were young adults, 96 percent of homes had a landline. Just 38 percent had cellphones. By 2013, 71 percent had a landline phone, and 89 percent had cellphones. Gen X moved from rotary dialing and push-button dialing to wireless, caller ID, call-waiting and inexpensive long distance.

26 Is Gen X into posting selfies?

Younger social media users are more likely to post selfies than older users, according to a 2015 Pennsylvania State University study. They also post different kinds. Teens aged 13-19 were more likely to post self-expressive content, including selfies on Instagram, than adults aged 25-39. The study found that teens' posts were tailored to earn likes in ways that older people's posts weren't. Teens showed moods and emotional states. A Pew report the year before said just 24 percent of Gen Xers had ever posted a selfie, compared with 55 percent of Millennials.

27 How does Gen X go online?

According to Nielsen, Gen X was checking out of laptops between 2015 and 2016 and going to tablets and smartphones. In fact, more Gen Xers had access to these devices than any other group except Millennials, who more frequently choose phones.

28 Is Gen X receptive to self-driving cars?

Not yet. In 2016, consumer research company J.D. Power asked this question. More than half the people younger than Generation X said they would trust self-driving technology. Gen X and older generations said they did not. The trust rate for Generation X was 41 percent. Twenty-seven percent said they definitely would not. Automakers need to win converts for self-driving cars to make it.

29 Is Generation X adopting smart home voice technology?

Yes. A 2017 study found that half of Gen Xers studied already owned home devices with voice-control features. Almost 80 percent said they want their next smart home devices to be voice activated. The top uses across all age groups were for entertainment, lighting, security and shopping. The findings come from a 2017 study by real estate company Coldwell Banker and smart home service provider Vivint.

News Media

30 Which media do Gen Xers rely on?

They use perhaps a wider mix of media than any other generation. According to Forrester Research, 48 percent listen to radio, 62 percent read newspapers and 85 percent have favorite TV shows. They are also into digital media. Millward Brown Digital reported that six in 10 use smartphones daily and three out of four regularly use online networks.

31 Where do Gen Xers get news about politics?

They are firmly between Boomers and Millennials. About 60 percent of Millennials said in a 2014 American Trends Panel survey that they get news about politics from Facebook. Sixty percent of Boomers said they get theirs from local TV. Then, results are flipped, with each getting just under 40 percent from the other generation's favorite source. Gen X is right in the middle, getting about half its political news from each of those sources.

32 Do Gen Xers trust the news media?

They trust some outlets but not others. They said in the 2014 American Trends study that they trusted these most: CNN, ABC News, NBC News, CBS News, MSNBC and PBS. Several print publications came next. Working from a list provided by researchers, respondents said they trusted these least: "The Rush Limbaugh Show," "The Glenn Beck Program," "The Sean Hannity Show," "The Daily Show" and "The Colbert Report." News shared among friends through social media is more trusted.

33 How much time do Gen Xers spend with social media?

A lot. In fact, their social media usage exceeds that of Millennials. Nielsen reported in 2017 that Gen X spends more time than any other generation on social media. Gen Xers spent almost seven hours a week with social media. Millennials spent just more than six.

34 Do news media overlook this generation?

That seems to be the case. Non-news companies don't talk about Gen X much, either. In 2015, CNBC analyzed companies' earnings calls with Wall Street analysts. It reviewed 17,776 transcripts. The words "Millennials," "Gen Y," "Generation Y" and "young adults" came up 620 times. There were 180 references to "Boomers," "Boomer" or "Baby Boom." Forgotten Generation X was mentioned just 16 times.

Pop Culture

35 What TV shows influenced Generation X?

TV gave Gen X two of its alternate names: the MTV Generation and the Latchkey Generation. They portray this as the first generation raised with after-school TV specials and music videos as babysitters. Development of educational programming like the existing "Sesame Street," "Mister Rogers' Neighborhood" and "Captain Kangaroo" gave rise to "Schoolhouse Rock." Youth variety shows included "Kids are People Too" and "Those Amazing Animals." "Dance Fever" was a precursor to reality shows such as "The Real World," "Survivor" and "The Bachelor." Top network shows of the '80s included "Cheers," "Roseanne," "Dallas," "The Cosby Show," "Murder She Wrote," "The Golden Girls," "Dynasty," "Who's the Boss?" and "Family Ties." The 1990s brought "Twin Peaks," "Northern Exposure, "Beverly Hills 90210," "Law & Order," "Dark Shadows," "The X-Files," "Buffy the Vampire Slayer," "Angel" and "Stargate SG-1." Cable's Fox, WB/UPN/CW and Spanish-language Univision and Telemundo challenged on-air networks CBS, ABC and NBC.

36 What was the significance of MTV?

MTV captured Gen X and changed entertainment. Not since the Beatles seized early Boomers in the 1960s had music achieved such a hold on young people. MTV launched early in the Gen X birth years, on Aug. 1, 1981, with the prophetic music video "Video Killed the Radio Star." By year's end, MTV had 2 million viewers. Its music video blocks gave Michael Jackson, Madonna and Duran Duran access to younger fans. Cabled into homes, music became an experience for the eyes as well as the ears. Michael Jackson's moonwalk video "Billie Jean," a single released early in 1983, brought MTV to mainstream audiences. For Gen Xers of a certain age, the day they got MTV was a milestone. MTV shattered network reluctance to air Black artists. MTV aired Jackson's full 14-minute version of the horror music video "Thriller" that December. With Prince, rappers Run-D.M.C. and others, MTV's audience grew. That exposure changed music. English synth-pop band Duran Duran brought high-quality 35mm music videos to MTV. The band led a second British music invasion from the early to mid 1980s. However, by ushering in livestreaming and the fragmentation of audiences for entertainment and news, MTV was also planting the seeds for its own decline.

37 How did videos influence music?

Music videos gave Michael Jackson and Madonna global audiences and spawned the phenomenon of hair and heavy-metal bands including Bon Jovi and Def Leppard. Madonna, Cyndi Lauper, Whitney Houston, Tina Turner and other women started fashion trends. They pushed the conversation on sexual liberation and gender politics. Run-D.M.C. is credited with taking rap mainstream. Part of that journey was its "Rock Box" video, the first rap video on MTV. "Yo! MTV Raps" opened the door for rappers to collaborate with Aerosmith on a 1986 "Walk This Way" that crossed genres and color lines.

Check out the Bias Busters' Gen X Playlist on Spotify:

https://open.spotify.com/user/paigejhannel/playlist/4wtHcoq01E1mtSSm16KXXk

Source: http://www.billboard.com/artists/top-100/1982?page=1

38 How did videos change music and film?

MTV pushed music productions to become much more visual and brought the world to suburban teens. When MTV started, most of its 24/7 schedule was clips from the United Kingdom, other parts of Europe and Australia. Demand for more and better video prompted the MTV Video Music Awards, starting in 1994. It launched filmmakers including David Fincher, Spike Jones, Michael Gondry, Julien

Temple and Tarsem Singh. Some won Oscars, Emmys and Golden Globes.

39 What was going on with movies for this generation?

Movies meant soundtracks, sequels, Stallone and Schwarzenegger. Movies and music rode the charts together. Prince's 1984 rock drama "Purple Rain" was the sixth highest selling sound track of all time and the movie made $220 million worldwide. The album was No. 1 on Billboard's Top 200 for 24 weeks straight. All five of its singles became worldwide hits. Other top '80s soundtracks included "The Blues Brothers" "Dirty Dancing," "Top Gun," "Chariots of Fire" and "Back to the Future."

Sylvester Stallone, with more than 80 movie credits, and Arnold Schwarzenegger, with more than 60, dominated theaters with tough-guy action movies through the 1980s. Their posters featured a bold name, a head shot and a big gun.

"Rocky" (Stallone)	1976
"Rocky II" (Stallone)	1979
"Rocky III" (Stallone)	1982
"Conan the Barbarian" (Schwarzenegger)	1982
"First Blood" (Stallone)	1982
"Conan the Destroyer" (Schwarzenegger)	1984
"The Terminator" (Schwarzenegger)	1984
"Rambo: First Blood Part II" (Stallone)	1985
"Rocky IV" (Stallone)	1985
"The Predator" (Schwarzenegger)	1987
"Rambo III" (Stallone)	1988
"Rocky V" (Stallone)	1990

"Terminator 2: Judgment Day" (Schwarzenegger) 1991

Other series of the time were "Star Wars" with its spinoff toys (1977, 1980, 1983, 1999, 2002, 2015, 2017)

"Friday the 13th"/ "Jason" (1980, 1981, 1982, 1984, 1985, 1986, 1988, 1989, 1993, 2001, 2003, 2009)

"Raiders of the Lost Ark" (1981, 1984, 1989, 2008)

"Beverly Hills Cop" (1984, 1987, 1994 …)

"Die Hard" (1988, 1990, 1995, 2007, 2013)

"Ghostbusters" (1984, 1989, 2016)

"Police Academy" (1984, 1985, 1986, 1987, 1988, 1989, 1994)

"Back to the Future" (1985, 1989, 1990)

Add in foreign films, the Sundance Film Festival and indie films. Writer/producer John Hughes' more than 50 films including "Sixteen candles," "The Breakfast Club," "Weird Science," "Ferris Bueller's Day Off" mirrored the generation.

40 What was the TV-music connection?

TV producers released soundtracks to promote shows. "Miami Vice" (1984-1990) fused music video and cops and carried fans from MTV to police shows. Series music director/curator became a job. CBS News' list of top 20 TV theme songs includes "Cheers," "The Simpsons," "The Fresh Prince of Bel-Air," "Full House," "Happy Days," "The Jeffersons" and "Laverne and Shirley."

41 What music was popular with young Gen Xers?

Pop, rock and dance music dominated Billboard's Top 100 lists. The era also saw the rise of hip hop or rap, Brit pop, and hair metal bands. Country music moved into the mainstream. Major pop duets included Kenny Rogers and Dolly Parton's "Islands in the Stream" and Diana Ross and Lionel Richie's "Endless Love." Popular, slickly produced tracks included work by Rick Astley, Bananarama and Kylie Minogue, and the English trio Stock Aitken Waterman. It was a time for synthesizers and drum machines, guitar solos and key changes. Other trends were grunge and punk.

42 What were the fashions?

Eighties fashions were big: big hair, oversized sweaters and big shoulder pads. Styles included pullovers and sweatshirts, logo clothing (Lacoste, Polo, Nike), acid-washed jeans and denim jackets with lots of pins and badges. The grunge phase brought big flannels and Doc Martens. There were the sneaker wars of Nike versus Reebok versus Air Jordan. Plastic shoes called jellies, anklet socks and leg warmers. Op (Ocean Pacific) and Jams branded clothing. Day-Glo colors with rubber bracelets. Scrunchies for hair, and mullet hairstyles. The mock turtleneck. Spandex miniskirts and the last era for prom dresses that still looked youth-appropriate with big puffy sleeves. "Cosby" sweaters, oversized blazers worn with stirrup pants. For men, Members Only jackets and parachute pants a la MC Hammer. The rock look with animal prints. The Michael Jackson red jacket from Thriller. Prince and Madonna's single lace glove. Movado and Swatch watches, and Ray-Ban Wayfarer sunglasses. The Official Preppy Handbook, released in 1980, showed polos with turned-up collars, madras shorts, sweaters knotted around the top and Docker and Sperry dock shoes without socks. Suburban malls gave rise to young-adult stores including Benetton, Esprit, The Limited, Express, Chess King, Banana Republic and J. Crew.

43 What did young Gen Xers read?

The 1983 New York Times bestseller list included Stephen King's "Pet Sematary," Judith Krantz's "Mistral's Daughter" and Umberto Eco's "The Name of the Rose." More recent bestsellers included John Irving's "Cider House Rules," Robert Ludlum's "The Bourne Supremacy," and novels by Danielle Steele. Comics played a big part in Gen X's upbringing, and not just Marvel and DC titles. It was the rise of the graphic novel, from Neil Gaiman's "Sandman" series to Art Spiegelman's "Maus." Books of newspaper comics included anthologies of "Doonesbury," "Garfield," "Bloom County," "Calvin & Hobbes" and "The Far Side."

44 How did cable affect sports coverage?

ESPN went live at 7 p.m. ET on Sept. 7, 1979, and Gen X grew up with 24-hour national and international sports coverage. In 1995, the cable network spent $10 million to launch the X Games. Their aerials and moguls entered the Olympics at the 1998 Winter Games at Nagano.

45 What were early Gen Xers' major U.S. professional sports stories?

- In the National Football League, Joe Montana led the San Francisco 49ers to Super Bowl championships in 1982, 1985, 1989 and 1990. The Washington Redskins and the Raiders each won twice in the decade. In the '90s, Dallas led with three Super Bowl wins.

- Michael Jordan was the National Basketball Association's most valuable player five times during the 1980s and '90s. Larry Bird and Magic Johnson were three-time MVPs. The Los Angeles Lakers, with Johnson and Kareem Abdul-Jabbar, and the Boston Celtics, with Bird and Kevin McHale, won almost every NBA title between 1980 and 1988.

- In the National Hockey League, the New York Islanders won the Stanley Cup in 1980-1983 and 1993, and the Edmonton Oilers, led by all-time leading scorer Wayne Gretzky, won in 1984, '85, '87, '88 and '90.

- The New York Yankees dominated Major League Baseball. Player Pete Rose was banned for life in 1989 for betting. Orioles "Iron Man" Cal Ripken broke Lou Gehrig's record for most consecutive games played. Ripken extended the record to 2,632 games.
- In boxing, Mike Tyson knocked out Michael Spinks in 91 seconds to win boxing's heavyweight championship in 1988. Tennis champions were John McEnroe, Andre Agassi, Martina Navratilova and Chris Evert-Lloyd.

46 What were college sports highlights?

Basketball's postseason March Madness tournament was expanded to 64 teams in 1985. The Patrick Ewing-led Georgetown Hoyas dominated the first half of the '80s. In 1992, an epic semifinal matchup of Duke versus Kentucky came down to "The Shot," a last-second half-court pass by Grant Hill to Christian Laettner to win, 104-103, as time ran out. Of note were the University of Michigan's Fab Five, coaches Rick Pitino and Mike Krzyzewski; and Coach Jim Valvano's "Don't give up ... Don't ever give up" speech. In football, Miami (Florida), won No. 1 rankings in 1983, 1987 and 1989, under three different head coaches.

47 What about international sports?

In the 1980 Winter Olympics at Lake Placid, New York, the U.S. men's hockey team came from trailing, 3-2, to beat the Soviet Union, 4-3, in the last 11 seconds. This was dubbed "The Miracle on Ice." The United States boycotted the summer games in Moscow that year over the invasion of Afghanistan. The Soviet Union then boycotted the 1984 summer games in Los Angeles. Most important in this Olympics era was figure skating and the Tonya Harding-Nancy Kerrigan showdown in 1994, and the Battle of the Brians (Boitano and Orser) and the Battle of the Carmens (Katerina Witt versus Debbie Thomas). In 1996 Muhammad Ali, shaking from Parkinson's, raised the torch at the opening ceremonies in Atlanta, and a pipe bomb killed one and hurt 111. Top gymnasts included Mary Lou Retton, Kerri Strug and Kurt Thomas. Swimmer Michael Phelps won eight gold medals in the 2008 Beijing games, eclipsing Mark Spitz's seven in 1972.

Contributions

48 Does this generation exhibit an entrepreneurial spirit?

Gen X is very entrepreneurial. Used to doing things on their own and with less college debt than younger people, Gen Xers have been twice as likely as Millennials to form startups. "Generations, Inc.," co-author Meagan Johnson wrote that entrepreneurship was set early for them. Growing up, many Gen Xers had to organize their time, figure things out on their own, do their chores and do their homework independently.

49 Who are some Gen X contributors?

There are too many to list, but several are in technology, which grew up with this generation. Two early ones were Michael Dell, born in 1965, founder and CEO of Dell, and Satya Nadella, 1967, CEO of Microsoft. Many are immigrants. Google founders Larry Page and Sergey Brin were born in 1973, which makes them Gen Xers. Uber co-founders Garrett Camp and Travis Kalanick are Gen Xers. Elon Musk, born in 1971, pioneered online payment and electric cars as the co-founder of PayPal and Tesla motors. He hopes to do the same for space travel with SpaceX. Twitter founder Jack Dorsey is a Gen Xer.

50 Who are Gen X leaders in business?

Lori Grenier, an entrepreneur famous as an investor on the show "Shark Tank," was born in 1969. Jeff Bezos of Amazon, the richest person in the world, is a Gen Xer. So is Sara Blakely of Spanx. Entertainers include Quentin Tarantino, Liz Phair, Will Smith, Jon Stewart, Jay-Z and Beyoncé. Facebook COO Sheryl Sandberg is an Xer. David Belle, born in 1973, created parkour. That style of moving rapidly around obstacles, typically in an urban space, has shaped cinema and movement.

51 Do Gen Xers support charities?

In 2013, Gen X represented 20 percent of total giving in the United States, according to a Giving Institute study. Half of Gen Xers surveyed said they would give more than once a year, more than other generations. Favorite causes include religious, social service and children's groups.

52 Do Gen Xers volunteer?

Nearly 30 percent volunteered in 2015, according to a study by the Corporation for National & Community Service. That is 19.9 million Gen X volunteers. The median time volunteered was 48 hours. Gen Xers preferred educational and religious organizations, according to this study. It showed that even though Generation X is smaller than the Baby Boom Generation, Gen X had more volunteers. However, Boomers were volunteering more hours, with a median of 6 hours a week. Millennials had fewer volunteers than Boomers or Xers both. Volunteering might have as much to do with age as with generational cohort. The generations were at different life stages when the survey was taken.

Education

53 What is the average educational level of Generation X?

Each generation has more education than the one before it, according to Pew. Generation X, though, is the first one in which women surpassed men for earning bachelor's degrees. This is from Pew's analysis of the Integrated Public Use Microdata Series' Current Population Survey of March, 2014:

	Bachelor's degrees	
	Men	Women
Silent	12%	7%
Boomer	17%	14%
Gen X	18%	20%
Millennial	20%	27%

54 What is the student debt load for Gen X?

Besides having more education than previous generations, Xers also have more college debt. This means many Gen Xers have higher incomes, but lower savings. Many struggle to pay for their children's college educations, which could push student loan burdens into the next generation. The Pew Charitable Trusts reported in 2014 that Gen Xers owe nearly six times what their parents owed at the same age.

Work

55 Do Gen Xers hold jobs longer than Millennials?

Because generations span 15-20 years, people in the same generation can be at very different life stages. A 20-year-old is not the same as a 35-year-old in the same generation. Bureau of Labor Statistics research shows that average job tenure for workers aged 25-34 hasn't changed much in 30 years. As people get older, they switch jobs less frequently. Older workers might feel that younger workers are moving all the time, but that is what they did at that age, too.

56 How long do Gen Xers tend to stay in one job?

In 2016, the job site LinkedIn reported that recent generations moved more than the ones before them. The study looked at graduates in five-year segments. It reported that late Gen Xers were more mobile than earlier ones at that same age. The study reported "People who graduated between 1986 and 1990 averaged more than 1.6 jobs, and people who graduated between 2006 and 2010 averaged nearly 2.85 jobs." However, this second period included the

Great Recession when a lot of people were cut. Not only did they have to find new jobs, they also learned that they needed to have a Plan B.

57 Are Gen Xers dedicated workers?

A global survey of more than 1,000 employers seems to support that. Futurestep found that more than half of respondents said Gen X was the most engaged in the workforce. Andrea Wolf, of Futurestep's human resources department, said Gen Xers place a much higher priority than Millennials on company culture and vision. She said Gen X cares less about work environment and more about contributing.

58 What do Gen Xers want in a job?

The Futurestep survey reported that the largest group of managers, 30 percent, said the most important thing to Gen X was to make a difference. That was twice as important as stability or opportunity. On the money side, pay and bonuses were twice as important as paid time off.

59 Are Gen Xers leaders or followers?

Fifty-one percent of today's workplace leaders come from this generation, according to the 2018 Global

Leadership Forecast from Development Dimensions
International, The Conference Board and EY. That
might catch people by surprise. The large number
of Boomers, who stay in the workforce longer than
prior generations, eclipsed the ascendance of Gen X.

60 Is there a Gen X leadership style?

Seventy percent of Gen X respondents told Center
for Talent Innovation researchers they want to be in
charge. Most said they want control over their work.
A report from the Society for Human Resource
Management said Gen Xers "work well in situations
where conditions are not well defined, or are
constantly changing." Their management style values
mentoring, helping others develop and letting people
do their jobs. They more frequently work across
divisions or seek outside ideas.

61 Do Gen Xers bridge Boomers and Millennials?

DDI said Gen Xers share several qualities with
neighboring generations. Like Boomers, they
exhibit loyalty, focus on education, identify and
develop talent. Xers are like Millennials in that they
are purpose-driven, eager to lead and have digital
know-how.

62 Is workplace equality improving for Gen X women?

The short answer is yes. Gender and generational differences expert Caroline Turner wrote that recent generations are getting more in tune with "what women have valued and needed." Turner wrote in the Huffington Post that Gen X "career moms" might be more receptive to having women in the workforce. Turner proposed this is growing with Millennials. They grew up seeing major strides in gender equality, such as a female presidential candidate.

63 Is the gender pay gap decreasing?

The gap was larger for Gen Xers than for Millennials according to a 2014 study by PayScale and Millennial Branding. That may be due to fluctuations in career stages, rather than progress. The pay gap for older Baby Boomers showed women making 2.7 percent less than men for comparable work. For Gen X women, it was 3.6 percent. Millennial women had a 2.2 percent disadvantage. The wage gap widened within all generations as responsibilities increased. For Gen X women, the gap grew from 3.6 percent to 7.4 percent. This was less than the wage disparity experienced by either Boomer or Millennial women.

64 How important are wages to workers?

A 2016 study by Paychex found money to be the No. 1 issue for Boomers, Gen Xers and Millennials. About 70 percent of Gen Xers and Millennials said low pay would make them leave. For Boomers, who were closer to retirement, 58 percent said they would leave over pay.

65 How important is work-life balance to Gen X?

The 2013 Regus Work-Life Balance Index indicated Gen Xers are more likely than Boomers to feel they are achieving at work. However, their "middle child" syndrome suggests they seek balance more than Boomers do, but feel more tied to companies than Millennials. Washington Post contributor Brigid Schulte wrote that there is overwhelming discontent over long hours. A key desire, especially for Millennials, is paid parental leave. Gen Xers fall somewhere between the fairly contented Boomers and the dissatisfied Millennials. For some Xers, the goal is not balance, but melding life with the workplace.

66 What other factors matter?

The chief difference between generations in the Paychex study was about overwork. The largest change is rising discontent over the feeling that employers just don't care. That concerned 37.7 percent of Boomers, 52.8 percent of Gen Xers and 54.5 percent of Millennials. Lack of recognition or reward was a concern for 46 percent of Gen Xers and Millennials, but not for as many Boomers.

Money

67 Do Gen Xers feel they will be financially secure?

Many are worried. A 2016 report by the Transamerica Center for Retirement found only 12 percent of Gen Xers were very confident that they will retire comfortably. Although average Gen X wages are higher than they were for Boomers, only 36 percent have more wealth. Financial security comes from accumulated wealth, not income.

68 How much do Gen X workers get paid?

The U.S. Bureau of Labor Statistics released these average annual incomes by age in the middle of 2018. Age brackets do not match generations exactly.

Baby Boomers
65 and older	$51,792
55-64	$51,636

Generation X
45-54	$51,272
35-44	$50,492

Millennials

25-34	$41,288
20-24	$28,080

Post-Millennials

16-19	$23,400

Individual incomes range widely according to geography, position, education, race, gender and many other factors. Comparing generations' wages at the same point in their careers would help, but would still be subject to those variations. What we can say reliably is that people are not earning or having more than their parents. Each generation has its own circumstances. For Gen X, the story is about recessions coming at key times. Although Gen Xers made more money than Boomers did at the same age, the Great Recession held them back. Housing values and the job market retreated just when many Gen Xers had gone to work and bought homes. As a group, they lost nearly half their wealth between 2007 and 2010, more than other generations.

69 Why don't Gen Xers save more?

The simple answer is that they have less to put away. Recessions and college debt hinder savings. Wage growth has slowed since the recession. Also, many Gen Xers now juggle taking care of their children and their parents. This prevents saving.

70 Is this "middle child" generation financially boxed in?

In some respects, yes, many Gen Xers are in a bind. The Transamerica report noted that, as pensions were phased out, Gen X was the first to have early access to 401(k) plans, which began in 1978. While 77 percent of Gen Xers are saving, they need to save more. About 30 percent had tapped into these retirement plans. Eighty-six percent of Xers worry that Social Security will not be there when they retire. They are concerned they will have to fund Social Security benefits for the larger Boomer and the Silent generations, while helping with college debt and loans for their children. By 2012, according to Pew, 42 percent of Gen Xers, more than any other generation, had parents over 65 and dependent children all at once. The squeeze could be hardest on people who have no siblings to share the burden.

71 Is there anything Gen X can do about this?

There could be. In 2016, Forbes published "Generation X's moment of power is almost here." It reported that "Gen X now has most of the managers in U.S. companies, is more entrepreneurial than Millennials at any age and is much more aggressive in starting new companies." The article said Gen X could be the dominant generation financially and politically by 2030.

Spending

72 How do Gen Xers spend their money?

The U.S. Department of Labor reports that about a third of Gen Xers' income goes for housing. About half goes for other expenses such as taxes, transportation, debt and utilities. Food at home is about 7 percent, leaving about 14 percent as disposable income.

73 Where does disposable income go?

This is for clothing, eating out and entertainment. Bloomberg BusinessWeek reported in 2016 that Gen Xers like to shop, though often for parents and children. Splurging means a trip to Pottery Barn or Home Depot, where smart home gadgets such as digital thermostats might be in the cart. Gen X, with the highest total income, also has the least disposable income.

Gen X and Millennial Food Trends

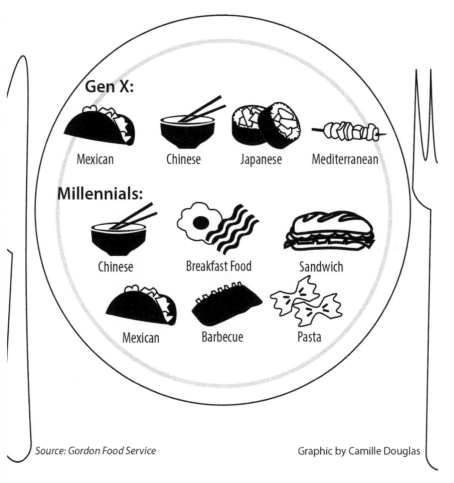

Gen X:

Mexican   Chinese   Japanese   Mediterranean

Millennials:

Chinese   Breakfast Food   Sandwich

Mexican   Barbecue   Pasta

Source: Gordon Food Service   Graphic by Camille Douglas

74 Has Gen X home ownership recovered from the 2008 recession?

Not entirely. In 2016, young Gen Xers represented the only segment of the U.S. population to show an increase in home ownership. Census data on home ownership was at 63.5 percent of the total adult population, lower than the 25-year average of 66.2 percent. The lone bright spot was people aged 35-44, where ownership rose 0.5 percent to 58.9 percent. Ownership for all other groups, including older Gen Xers, was down slightly. A 2016 Wall Street Journal analysis of federal housing data said home ownership for Generation X could remain depressed for years. When asked by Forbes, Gen Xers said their top financial regret was that they had not stretched to buy a home.

75 Do Gen Xers gravitate toward certain states?

They live everywhere, of course, and a 2017 analysis by Governing.com found hotspots. Georgia and New Jersey had the highest concentrations. The Great Plains, especially the Dakotas, had the lowest. North Dakota and Florida had the fastest growing Gen X populations, while Illinois was declining.

76 Does Gen X buy cars?

Generation X buys more cars per capita than other generations. TrueCar.com has said that Gen Xers with children go for practicality, spaciousness and safety. They prefer models with three rows of seats, such as some SUVs and minivans. On-board technology is a priority

77 How does Generation X bank?

Gen Xers bank more like Millennials than like Boomers. Financial services company BAI studied this in 2015. It found that each generation banked in many ways, but had preferences. For Gen Xers, online and mobile phone banking were equally popular. Millennials preferred mobile banking. Boomers preferred to go into the bank. In no generation, though, did any single method capture even 30 percent of preferences.

Politics

78 How does Gen X identify politically?

The divide in U.S. politics is between left-leaning Gen X and Millennials and the right-leaning Baby Boom and Greatest generations. A 2017 Pew Research report said that the largest growth is among younger, liberal Democrats and older, conservative Republicans. All generations reported similar concentrations of moderates.

79 Does Gen X vote?

Potential voters are citizens of voting age, eligible voters or those who registered and actual voters go to the polls. Turnout is the percentage of registered voters who vote. Gen X and younger voters have had more eligible voters than groups over 54 since the 2016 election, but they vote less. Pew Research reported, "In general, as a generation ages, turnout rises, hits a peak, and then declines." For their age, Gen X and younger voters have not voted as much as older generations. These are pople's "yes" responses to Pew questions about whether they had voted.

	1996	2000	2004	2008	2012	2016
Silent	69%	70%	72%	70%	72%	70%
Boomer	60%	64%	69%	69%	69%	69%
Gen X	41%	47%	57%	61%	61%	63%
Millennial			46%	50%	46%	49%

80 How does Gen X vote in presidential elections?

CNN exit polls on Election Day 2016 showed that this age group was divided at right around half for Donald Trump and half for Hillary Clinton. Trump's biggest support came from people over 50. Clinton's came from people under 30. In 2016, Clinton received 48.2 percent of the popular vote. Trump received 46.1 percent but won the electoral vote.

81 How does Gen X view government?

In 2017, Pew found that more Gen Xers than Boomers or Silents preferred bigger government. Half of Gen Xers said they would rather have a bigger government. Forty-three percent of Baby Boomers surveyed and 30 percent of those in the Silent Generation agreed. On another issue, 57 percent of Millennials and 53 percent of Xers said government does not do enough for younger people. In contrast, almost half of Boomers and just more than a third of Silents agreed with that.

82 Where is Gen X on environmental issues?

One study characterizes Gen X as uninformed and unconcerned about climate change. Jon D. Miller directs the University of Michigan's Longitudinal Study of American Youth. His "Generation X Report" said most Gen Xers are disengaged, dismissive or doubtful about environmental issues. Furthermore, attention and concern went down from 2009 to 2011.

83 Does Gen X accept same-sex marriage?

According to the Pew Research Center, each new generation has been more accepting of same-sex marriages than the prior one. Also, acceptance is growing within each generation. Approval rates looked like this in 2017:

Millennials	73%
Generation X	65%
Baby Boomers	56%
Silent Generation	41%

84 Will we ever see a Gen Xer in the White House?

It can still happen. When Donald Trump became president in 2017 at age 70, the country was on course for 28 or 32 years of Boomer presidents. That is longer than the span of years in which

Boomers were born. The Greatest Generation, born in 1928-1945, never had a president. By 2020, early Millennials will be old enough to be president and all will be eligible to vote. But the youngest Gen Xers still will have 30 more years before they turn 70. Several sought the Republican presidential nomination in 2016. Gen X leaders in other countries have included Canadian Prime Minister Justin Trudeau, French President Emmanuel Macron, Mexican President Enrique Peña Nieto, New Zealand Prime Minister Jacinda Ardern, Belgium Prime Minister Charles Michel and Colombian President Iván Duque Márquez.

85 How well is Gen X represented in the U.S. Congress?

In the 2019-2020 U.S. House, Gen X increased its number of seats from 118 to 138. This was a 17 percent increase in the 435-seat body. However, representation was still below Gen X's percentage in the population over 25, the minimum age to be elected to the House.

Families

86 Are Gen X women waiting to have children?

This generation had the greatest change in the age at which women had their first child. The first Gen Xers were born in 1965 and, on average, started having children in the 1980s. According to the Centers for Disease Control and Prevention, the mean age for first-time mothers increased from 21.4 in 1970 to 25.0 years in 2006. The Center for Work Life Policy reported that Gen Xers are also less likely than prior generations to have children. More than 40 percent of women aged 41-45 told researchers they had not had children.

87 Does Gen X have more single parents?

Actually, the frequency of single-parent households grew faster before and after Gen X. The proportion of children living in one-parent homes has grown from about 9 percent in 1960 to 26 percent in 2014. According to a Pew Research analysis of Census data, the number plateaued around 20 percent from 1980 to 2000. This is when many Gen Xers were having children. Single-parent families increased again with Millennials. This has been attributed to money concerns and more college-educated career women postponing motherhood or having fewer children.

88 What is the average family size for Gen X parents?

Generation X and Millennials have changed the definition of family, so this number requires interpretation. Many households now are just one or two adults. Some have multiple generations or unrelated people. A better measure might be the U.S. fertility rate, which is the average number of children women have. That number was 2.91 and declining the year the first Gen Xer was born in 1965. Since 1985, when Gen X started turning 20, the fertility rate has been much lower, between 1.84 births and 2.08.

89 Are Gen X parents overprotective?

Let's just call them very involved. This might be because of a desire to be more present in their children's lives than their parents were in theirs. Xers experienced the rise in divorced parents and two-income families. Experience might have turned these latchkey kids into helicopter parents.

90 Where are Gen Xers with divorce?

Divorces had a historic rise while Gen Xers were being born. It went from about 10 per 1,000 married women in 1965 to almost 23 in 1980, when most Gen Xers were barely teenagers. Since then, and as Gen Xers have gotten married, the divorce rate has steadily declined. In 2015, the divorce rate was 16.9 per 1,000. That was the lowest rate in 40 years. Some reasons for the decline are that more couples were unmarried, the marriage age had risen and couples waited longer to get divorced.

91 Are Gen Xers' adult children more likely to live with them?

Gen X has entered the perfect storm that some younger Boomers are weathering. These are the dynamics: some children have not moved out, older children are coming back and Mom and Dad are moving in. This comes from the National Association of Realtors' 2017 Home Buyers and Sellers Generational Trends Report. According to Investopedia, "The sandwich generation is the generation of middle-aged individuals who are pressured to support both aging parents and growing children." Forty-seven percent of people in their 40s and 50s are taking care of their children, including financially supporting them, while also taking care of parents.

Health

92 What are life expectations and expectancies for Gen X?

Fifty-three percent of Gen Xers said in a 2017 MDVIP.com study that they want to live past 90. Twenty-five percent said they hope to make 100. When early Generation Xers were born, the Centers for Disease Control and Prevention put their life expectancy at 70.2 years. For people born in 1980, it had risen to 73.7 years. That was about the transition point from Gen X to Millennials. In 2016, the Centers for Disease Control and Prevention reduced life expectancies for Americans overall from 78.9 to 78.8 years. That was the first rollback in 20 years. This could be a wakeup call for Gen Xers who want to live long and prosper.

93 Do Gen Xers take care of themselves?

For people who want to live a long time, they could do better. MDVIP.com found that only half of Gen Xers had received an annual physical in the prior year. The figure for Millennials was 72 percent. Some Gen Xers said they don't go to the doctor because they don't want to hear bad news. Some who did see doctors said following orders is a low-priority hassle. Two-thirds admitted they should eat better, lose weight, exercise more and manage stress.

94 What health issues characterize Gen X?

Diabetes is up for Gen Xers, according to the 2014 National Diabetes Statistics Report. Rutgers' Robert Wood Johnson Medical School reported that Gen Xers are more likely than Boomers to have strokes. This was attributed to obesity and diabetes, risk factors for cardiovascular disease. Obesity and diet are suspected in higher colon and rectal cancer rates for Gen X. High blood pressure and mental health issues were also cited.

95 How do Gen Xers compare on fitness?

According to the Centers for Disease Control and Prevention, 40.2 percent of adults aged 40-59 in 2011-2014 were obese, the highest rate of any age group. Most were in Generation X. The study did not blame generational membership or predict about whether Millennials will wind up there, too

96 Is Gen X physically active?

Middle Gen Xers grew up seeing Jane Fonda and Olivia Newton-John become fitness icons. They saw the rising popularity of aerobics, Pilates, barre, yoga and CrossFit. Shows like "The Biggest Loser" targeted this age range as contestants. According to the 2016 Physical Activity Council Report, 31 percent of Gen Xers are inactive. About 48 percent of Gen Xers reported participating in a fitness activity once a week. Among active individuals, 66.2 percent participated in fitness sports and 51.4 percent did outdoor activities such as camping, swimming for fitness, bicycling and hiking.

97 What about Gen X's mental health?

The American Psychological Association's 2018 edition of "Stress in America" described Gen Xers as reporting more stress than prior generations, but less than younger ones. Stressors included work, money, the state of the nation, political discord and discrimination. A study in the 2017 Psychiatric Services journal described late Boomers and early Gen Xers as having higher risk for unreported serious mental distress. This includes depression, anxiety and bipolar disorder. Researchers cite the Great Recession as a stressor.

Recreation

98 How do Gen Xers spend their free time?

These were top leisure activities for Gen Xers, according to a Harris poll:

Watching TV	45%
Reading	35%
Computer/internet	19%
Family and friends	19%
Watching movies	13%
Working out	12%
Walking/running	11%
Gaming	10%
Listening to/playing music	9%
Shopping	7%

99 Are Gen Xers active in social groups?

Yes, though not the kinds their parents liked. They participate in parent-teacher organizations, youth sports clubs, book clubs and community organizations. Community lunch and breakfast groups are out. This comes from a study by the University of Michigan's Institute for Social Research.

100 Does Gen X like to travel?

According to the Sabre Travel Network, Gen X spends slightly more on travel than Millennials or Boomers. Seventy-nine percent was for pleasure, according to the Shullman Research Center. The emphasis was on family travel.

Gen X Significant Events

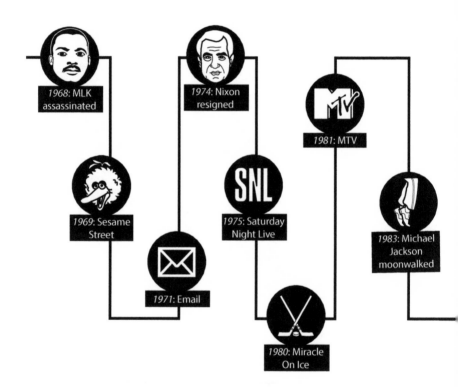

- 1968: MLK assassinated
- 1969: Sesame Street
- 1971: Email
- 1974: Nixon resigned
- 1975: Saturday Night Live
- 1980: Miracle On Ice
- 1981: MTV
- 1983: Michael Jackson moonwalked

Source: Pew Research Center "Modern historic events by generation"

Millennial Defining Moments

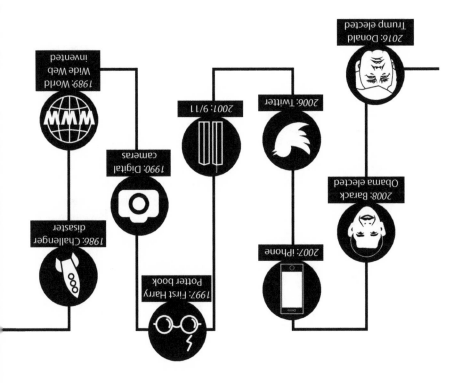

1986: Challenger disaster

1989: World Wide Web invented

1990: Digital cameras

1997: First Harry Potter book

2001: 9/11

2006: Twitter

2007: iPhone

2008: Barack Obama elected

2016: Donald Trump elected

Related Books

100 Questions and Answers About Gender Identity
Michigan State University School of Journalism, 2017
The guide is written for anyone who wants quick answers to basic, introductory questions about transgender people. It is a starting point people who want to get a fast grounding in the facts.
http://news.jrn.msu.edu/culturalcompetence/

ISBN: 978-1-641800-02-0

100 Questions and Answers About Sexual Orientation
Michigan State University School of Journalism, 2018
This guide has sections on terminology, identity, relationships, families, health, safety, school, work, visibility, coming out, civil rights, politics and religion.
http://news.jrn.msu.edu/culturalcompetence/

ISBN: 978-1-641800-27-3

100 Questions and Answers About Chaldean Americans
Michigan State University School of Journalism 2019
This guide has sections on identity, language, religion, culture, customs, social norms, economics, politics, education, work, families and food. It is written for those who want authoritative answers to basic, questions about this immigrant group from Iraq.

ISBN: 978-1-934879-63-4

Print and ebooks available on Amazon.com and other retailers.

Related Books

100 Questions and Answers About Muslim Americans
Michigan State University School of Journalism, 2014
This guide was done at a time of rising intolerance in
the United States toward Muslims. The guide describes
the presence of this religious group around the world
and inside the United States. It includes audio on
how to pronounce some basic Muslim words.
http://news.jrn.msu.edu/culturalcompetence/

ISBN: 978-1-939880-79-6

100 Questions and Answers About African Americans
Michigan State University School of Journalism, 2016
Learn about the racial issues that W.E.B. DuBois said in
1900 would be the big challenge for the 20th century.
This guide explores Black and African American identity,
history, language, contributions and more. Learn more
about current issues in American cities and campuses.
http://news.jrn.msu.edu/culturalcompetence/

ISBN: 978-1-942011-19-4

100 Questions and Answers About Immigrants to the U.S.
Michigan State University School of Journalism 2016
This simple, introductory guide answers 100 of the
basic questions people ask about U.S. immigrants
and immigration in everyday conversation. It
has answers about identity, language, religion,
culture, customs, social norms, economics,
politics, education, work, families and food.

ISBN: 978-1-934879-63-4

100 Questions and Answers about Police Officers
Michigan State University School of Journalism 2018
This simple, introductory guide answers 100 of the
basic questions people ask about police officers,
sheriff's deputies, public safety officers and tribal
police. It focuses on policing at the local level,
where procedures vary from coast to coast. The
guide includes a resource about traffic stops.

ISBN: 978-1-64180-013-6

Print and ebooks available on Amazon.com and other retailers.

Related Books

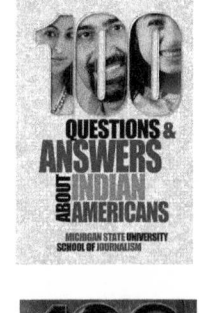

100 Questions and Answers About Indian Americans
Michigan State University School of Journalism, 2013
In answering questions about Indian Americans, this guide also addresses Pakistanis, Bangladeshis and others from South Asia. The guide covers religion, issues of history, colonization and national partitioning, offshoring and immigration, income, education, language and family.
http://news.jrn.msu.edu/culturalcompetence/

ISBN: 978-1-939880-00-0 m

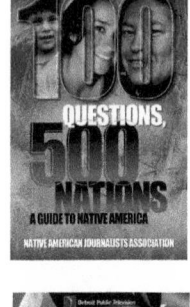

100 Questions, 500 Nations: A Guide to Native America
Michigan State University School of Journalism, 2014
This guide was created in partnership with the Native American Journalists Association. The guide covers tribal sovereignty, treaties and gaming, in addition to answers about population, religion, U.S. policies and politics. The guide includes the list of federally recognized tribes.
http://news.jrn.msu.edu/culturalcompetence/

ISBN: 978-1-939880-38-3

100 Questions and Answers About Veterans
Michigan State University School of Journalism, 2015
This guide treats the more than 20 million U.S. military veterans as a cultural group with distinctive training, experiences and jargon. Graphics depict attitudes, adjustment challenges, rank, income and demographics. Includes six video interviews by Detroit Public Television.
http://news.jrn.msu.edu/culturalcompetence/

ISBN: 978-1-942011-00-2

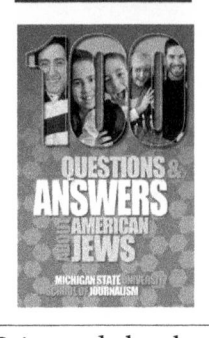

100 Questions and Answers About American Jews
Michigan State University School of Journalism 2016
We begin by asking and answering what it means to be Jewish in America. The answers to these wide-ranging, base-level questions will ground most people and set them up for meaningful conversations with Jewish acquaintances.
http://news.jrn.msu.edu/culturalcompetence/

ISBN: 978-1-942011-22-4

Print and ebooks available on Amazon.com and other retailers.

Related Books

100 Questions and Answers About Americans
Michigan State University School of Journalism, 2013
This guide answers some of the first questions asked by newcomers to the United States. Questions represent dozens of nationalities coming from Africa, Asia, Australia, Europe and North and South America. Good for international students, guests and new immigrants.
http://news.jrn.msu.edu/culturalcompetence/

ISBN: 978-1-939880-20-8

100 Questions and Answers About Arab Americans
Michigan State University School of Journalism, 2014
The terror attacks of Sept. 11, 2001, propelled these Americans into a difficult position where they are victimized twice. The guide addresses stereotypes, bias and misinformation. Key subjects are origins, religion, language and customs. A map shows places of national origin.
http://news.jrn.msu.edu/culturalcompetence/

ISBN: 978-1-939880-56-7

100 Questions and Answers About East Asian Cultures
Michigan State University School of Journalism, 2014
Large university enrollments from Asia prompted this guide as an aid for understanding cultural differences. The focus is on people from China, Japan, Korea and Taiwan and includes Mongolia, Hong Kong and Macau. The guide includes history, language, values, religion, foods and more.
http://news.jrn.msu.edu/culturalcompetence/

ISBN: 978-939880-50-5

100 Questions and Answers About Hispanics & Latinos
Michigan State University School of Journalism, 2014
This group became the largest ethnic minority in the United States in 2014 and this guide answers many of the basic questions about it. Questions were suggested by Hispanics and Latinos. Includes maps and charts on origin and size of various Hispanic populations.
http://news.jrn.msu.edu/culturalcompetence/

ISBN: 978-1-939880-44-4

Print and ebooks available on Amazon.com and other retailers.

Our Story

The 100 Questions and Answers series springs from the idea that good journalism should increase cross-cultural competence and understanding. Most of our guides are created by Michigan State University journalism students.

We use journalistic interviews to surface the simple, everyday questions that people have about each other but might be afraid to ask. We use research and reporting to get the answers and then put them where people can find them, read them and learn about each other.

These cultural competence guides are meant to be conversation starters. We want people to use these guides to get some baseline understanding and to feel comfortable asking more questions. We put a resources section in every guide we make and we arrange community conversations. While the guides can answer questions in private, they are meant to spark discussions.

Making these has taught us that people are not that different from each other. People share more similarities than differences. We all want the same things for ourselves and for our families. We want to be accepted, respected and understood.

Please email your thoughts and suggestions to Series Editor Joe Grimm at joe.grimm@gmail.com, at the Michigan State University School of Journalism.

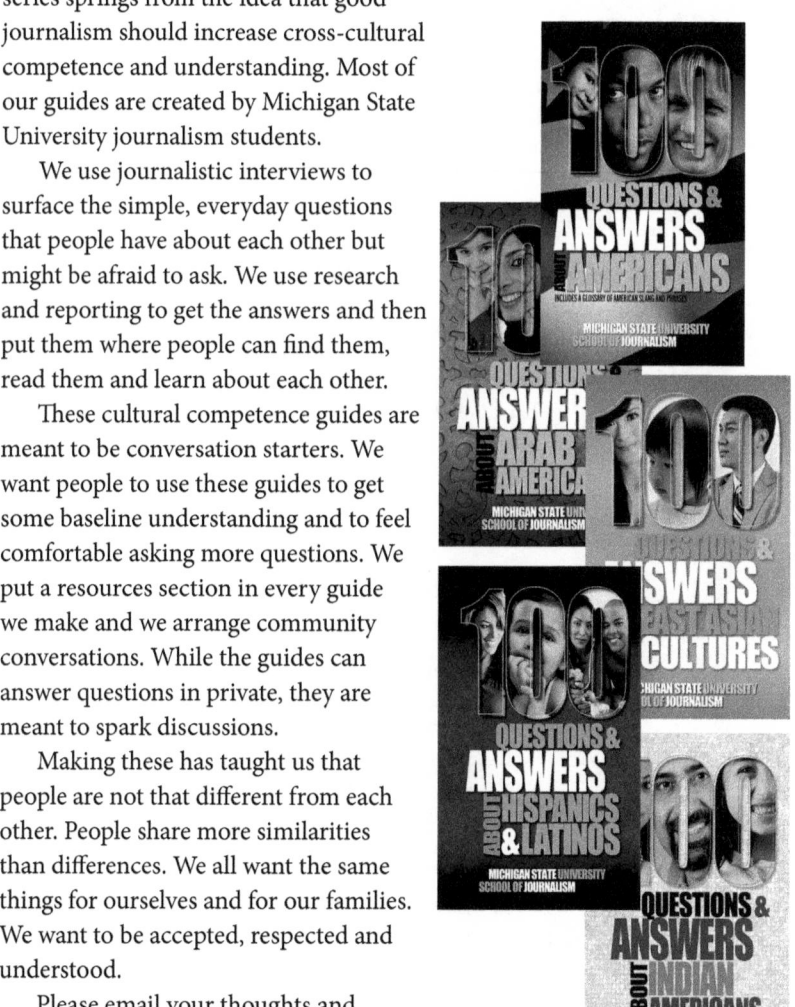

http://news.jrn.msu.edu/culturalcompetence

CPSIA information can be obtained
at www.ICGtesting.com
Printed in the USA
FFHW021531280519
52705181-58201FF

100 Questions and Answers About Millennials

Forged by economics, technology, pop culture and work

**Michigan State University
School of Journalism**

Front Edge Publishing

For more information and further discussion, visit
news.jrn.msu.edu/culturalcompetence/

Cover art and design by
Rick Nease
www.RickNeaseArt.com

Published by
Front Edge Publishing, LLC
42015 Ford Road, Suite 234
Canton, Michigan

Front Edge Publishing specializes in speed and flexibility
in adapting and updating our books. We can include
links to video and other online media. We offer discounts
on bulk purchases for special events, corporate training,
and small groups. We are able to customize bulk orders
by adding corporate or event logos on the cover and
we can include additional pages inside describing your
event or corporation. For more information about our
fast and flexible publishing or permission to use our
materials, please contact Front Edge Publishing at info@
FrontEdgePublishing.com.

Contents

Preface

Generations are at a key transition point—once again.

In June 2015, the U.S. Census Bureau declared that the nation's population of Millennials had surpassed Baby Boomers. Later, the bureau announced that this would actually happen in 2019. What's going on? Did the Census Bureau miscount? Not really. The Census Bureau counts people. Generations are determined by a wider array of demographers, social scientists and marketers. They try to use generational markers to group people by similarities. In 2018, Pew Research Center President Michael Dimock wrote that the nonpartisan organization had nailed down the end of Millennial birth years as 1996. He explained that parsing the population into generations "can provide a way to understand how different formative experiences (such as world events and technological, economic and social shifts) interact with the life-cycle and aging process to shape people's views of the world."

Dimock noted that the oldest Millennials, with a birth year of 1981, were well into adulthood at 37 and that keeping the generation at 16 years, comparable

to Gen X, made sense. But divisions are not always this arbitrary. Clear changes in the birth rate set the Baby Boom generation at 19 years. Formative events that Dimock noted for Millennials included the 2001 terror attacks, wars in Iraq and Afghanistan, polarized politics, diversity, the election of the nation's first Black president, the Great Recession and technology.

Post-Millennials, their label and birth years still undecided, are being defined by having grown up in a post-9/11 world with 24-7 cellphone connectivity and social media.

This is the first double book in this Michigan State University series of guides to cultural competence. We combined generations because they are largely described in relation to each other. To describe one, we compare it to others. Generation X and Millennials are a good pairing because of their growing power. We cover them separately because, though they are connected, they are distinct. Each has its own realities and stereotypes.

It would be a gross oversimplification to believe people born at the end of one generation are like those who came 15 years before them and are different than those born the next year. Parents know that siblings, born in the same generation and raised in the same household, can be like night and day.

Many people disown generational labels, finding more in common with other cohorts. The labels often are imposed by older people, the ones who sigh, "What's the matter with kids today?"

And there are the stereotypes: Slackers. Hippies. Workaholics. Job hoppers. Techies. Every generation has its stereotypes. But seeing the world in generations is a handy—perhaps necessary—first step to begin

to understand people's values, goals and needs. Compartmentalizing also recognizes that the world does not change in a steady continuum, but in fits and starts with great advances and, sometimes, reassessment.

Employers and educators use generational boxes to understand workers and students. Marketers and advertisers use the work of researchers to sell goods and services. In a world where it takes a lot of work to get to understand people individually, generational thinking is a shortcut to reaching millions with the fewest messages.

However, stereotyping people can have grave consequences in lost opportunity, employee turnover and diminished creativity. Unlocking the answers to running a workplace in which four generations collaborate is a holy grail that would increase a company's value dramatically at very little cost. It would also make work so much more rewarding. The hazard in generational shorthand is that it also creates misunderstanding. The smart strategy is to use generational characteristics to understand context and background, but to get to know people as the individuals they are.

Joe Grimm
Series editor
School of Journalism
Michigan State University

Demographics

1 Who are the Millennials?

People born from the very early 1980s to the mid 1990s are, by most definitions, Millennials. However, generations do not always have crisp edges. Baby Boomers were an exception, bracketed by a sharp upturn and downtick in the U.S. birth rate. With most generations, different demographers give different dates. Furthermore, people in the same generation do not all share the same perspectives. People born near the beginning or end of a generation are called "cuspers," and may have characteristics of another generation.

2 How many Millennials are there in the United States?

The United States has 73 million Millennials. They succeed Baby Boomers as the largest living generation and will be surpassed by the post-Millennials.

3 How many Millennials are there in the world?

The Pew Research Center estimates there are 2 billion Millennials in the world, about 27 percent of the global population. But don't get carried away. Generations are not monolithic. Formative experiences vary from year to year, continent to continent and person to person. Not all countries pay a lot of attention to generations. With varied political, social and economic transition points, generational breaks happen at different times in different places. Using United Nations' birth data for 1980-2000, Bloomberg has estimated that the post-Millennial generation will comprise 32 percent of the world's population of 7.7 billion in 2019. That would exceed Millennials.

4 What else are Millennials called?

Other names include the Net Generation and the Internet Generation or iGen, referring to their experience growing up as digital natives. That term means they were born into a world with internet access. More names are Linksters, the Selfie Generation and the Rainbow Generation. Generation Y has also been used, following Generation X. The winner, Millennials, means the first people to come of age in the new millennium. Historian, author, economist and demographer Neil Howe is credited with coining "Millennial Generation."

5 Why was Rainbow Generation suggested?

The Brookings Institution calls diversity the defining characteristic of this group. It predicted Millennials will be key in the journey to becoming a nation in which there is no racial or ethnic majority. Forty-four percent of Millennials were non-White in 2018. The Census Bureau projects that, as the U.S. population grows from 2020 to 2060, the White-alone population will shrink from 199 million to 179 million.

6 Are interracial relationships more common among Millennials?

One in six newlywed couples were multiracial, according to a 2017 Pew analysis of Census data. This has led to more multiracial babies. Pew reported that this number had already risen from 1 percent in 1970 to 10 percent in 2013. Pew also reported that acceptance for interracial marriage is greater among Millennials than with any other generation. Eighty-five percent of Millennials said they would be fine marrying someone of another race. The Gallup polling organization also found that more Americans than ever approve of interracial marriages. Most respondents said they would approve of their child or grandchild marrying someone of another race.

7 Are LGBTQ+ people part of this rainbow?

Here, too, Millennials are changing the country. Millennials are almost twice as likely as the overall U.S. population to identify as LGBT, according to a 2017 Gallup report. While 4 percent of the overall U.S. population identified as LGBT, 7.3 percent of people born from 1980 and 1998 identified that way. This was up from 5.8 percent for that age group in 2012.

8 What traits are attributed to Millennials?

Gallup described Millennials as either "technology savvy or highly-indebted narcissists." In 2015, Pew asked Millennials which labels they would choose for themselves. Thirty-nine percent chose idealistic. Thirty-five percent said entrepreneurial. Forty percent chose environmentally conscious. And 36 percent said hard working. Negative descriptors included being more self-absorbed, wasteful, greedy and cynical than prior generations.

9 Where do Millennials live?

Changing residential patterns are remaking U.S. communities. A University of Virginia study of Census data from 1990 to 2015 found that Millennials, largely raised in suburbs, were moving to cities. CNN reported that the shift was reviving

cities and hurting farther-out communities.

According to Realtor.com, top cities for home-buying Millennials in 2017 were Salt Lake City, Miami, Orlando, Seattle, Houston, Los Angeles, Buffalo, Albany, San Francisco and San Jose. A Forbes article called Alexandria, Virginia, a Millennial boomtown.

Technology

10 At what age did Millennials receive cellphones and computers?

Even very young children learn to swipe their way through apps. Computers and tablets generally come before cellphones. Those come when children are mobile and parents let them have the devices. That age has been pushed younger. Clearly, though, the devices have been everywhere for Millennials' entire lives. Not all Gen Xers grew up with them.

11 Which is Millennials' preferred device?

Pew's 2017 Mobile Fact Sheet showed that 100 percent of people aged 18-24 that it asked owned cellphones. Ninety-two percent had smartphones. Pew also found that 17 percent of adults aged 18 to 24 depend on their smartphones for internet connection—the highest percentage of all adult categories. Yet, according to AdWeek, 35 percent of Millennials preferred laptops and desktops, while 27 percent preferred phones.

Nine Apps Most Commonly used by Millennials

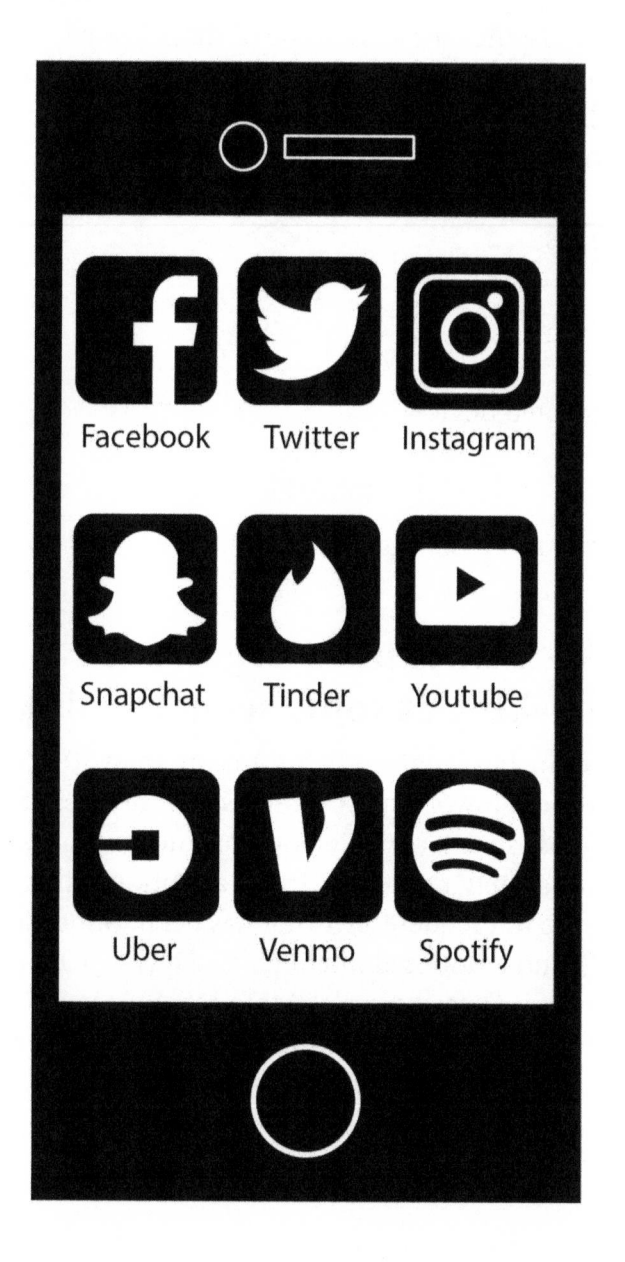

12 How much time do Millennials spend with technology?

Research disputes the stereotype of them always being on their devices. A Nielsen study in 2017 found that Millennials were online less than either Gen X or Boomers. These were the weekly usage times in hours and minutes that Nielsen reported for Millennials:

TV	19:18
Smartphone	17:49
Radio	10:40
TV-connected device	7:16
PC	5:53
Tablet	3:05

People use more than one device at a time.

13 Are Millennials as good at multitasking as some seem to think?

Multitasking has been studied for more than 50 years. Although working several tasks or devices at once sounds smart, a whole body of studies shows we do things better when we focus attention rather than divide it. Frequent pivoting has been found to lower IQ and emotional intelligence. Devora Zack, author of "Singletasking: Get More Done—One Thing at a Time," wrote that multitasking can reduce productivity by 40 percent.

14 Do Millennials really have shorter attention spans than goldfish?

The story that the Millennial attention span is eight seconds, a half second less than goldfish, comes from a Microsoft study done in Canada for marketers. The study has problems. It was tiny: 2,000 in an online survey and 112 measured by electroencephalograph. The study was not peer reviewed. Attention was ill-defined. The goldfish data was not explained. The authors did not claim a significant generational difference in attention spans. But the story persists. Here is a more revealing fact: In 2017 the National Basketball Association said it was going to speed up games to make them more appealing to Millennials. And goldfish.

15 Are Millennials bad at face-to-face communication?

A study found that about 80 percent of Millennials and 78 percent of Gen Xers prefer to communicate in person. Millennials use instant messaging and texting, but prefer face-to-face. The study was by the USC Marshall School of Business, the London Business School and PricewaterhouseCoopers. In contrast to the goldfish study, this one looked at 40,000 people in 22 countries.

16 How do Millennials relate to technology?

In "Are Millennials Falling Out of Love with Technology?" Wired magazine reported that 86 percent of Millennials said technology makes life simpler. Sixty-nine percent said it enhances their personal relationships. On the other hand, about 60 percent said society relies too much on technology and that it dehumanizes society. According to Pew, Millennials both benefit and suffer from technology. Some predicted that the thirst for instant gratification will lead them to make "quick and shallow choices."

17 Do Millennials prefer phones for texting, or talking?

A 2014 Gallup poll found that text messages outranked calls as the dominant form of communication among Millennials. There are two reasons for this, according to a Forbes article by Neil Howe. Phone calls can seem intrusive or presumptuous. Texts let the receiver decide when to handle them. Also, task-oriented Millennials will "default to whichever communication method will help them complete their to-do lists most efficiently." Incidentally, the first text was sent on Dec. 3, 1992.

18 Which social media platforms do Millennials prefer?

Pew reports that 86 percent of adults ages 18 to 29 use social media. As of April 2016, 88 percent of adults ages 18 to 29 used Facebook. Fifty-nine percent used Instagram. Pinterest, Twitter and LinkedIn were all about 35 percent.

19 Do Millennials prefer CDs or downloads?

In a study of 1,300 Millennials' shopping habits, the Intelligence Group found that a little more than one-third made only "necessary" purchases. Millennials value access over ownership. An example is choosing Spotify and Netflix memberships over physical CDs. This extends to other services that do not require major financial commitments.

20 Do Millennials read books?

By a clear margin, Millennials read more books than other generations. They also read more books than Gen X did at their age. Pew found in 2016 that the 18-29 age group was the one most likely to have read any sort of book in the prior year. Eighty percent said they had. That compared to 73 percent in the 30-49 group, 70 percent of 50- to 64-year-olds, and 67 percent of older people. Also, a study for the trade journal Publishing Perspectives of 1,000 Millennials found that people 18-34 were nearly twice as likely

to have read a book in print than on a digital device. Print readership was 79 percent. Tablets were next at 46 percent.

Money

21 How did the Great Recession affect Millennials?

The 2007-2009 Great Recession and the years after hit millions of Millennials at a critical time in their financial lives. It hurt more than just their income. It caused debt and delayed home ownership, which limited wealth accumulation. A 2018 report by the Federal Reserve Bank of St. Louis said some Millennials might never recover. People in their late 20s to early 30s continued to lose ground after the Great Recession, from 2010 to 2016. As other generations recovered, the wealth gap between young and old grew. According to the St. Louis study "A Lost Generation," the net worth of families headed by early Millennials was 34 percent below what had been expected.

22 Have Millennial incomes recovered?

Wages for a household headed by a Millennial male in 2014 were more than 10 percent less in real dollars than for a Boomer household in the comparable year of 1978. This comes from a 2018 Federal Reserve Board report.

23 How are households headed by women?

These experienced a similar dip. The Fed reported that the median earnings of female-headed Millennial households in 2014 were about 3 percent lower than those of comparable Gen X households in 1998. However, Millennial women started several trends that could help. They are marrying later, having children later, attending school more and saving more. All build wealth.

24 Where is Millennial wealth now?

The Fed report said the average real net worth of Millennial households in 2016 was 20 percent less than Baby Boomers had in the comparable year of 1989. Millennials were 40 percent behind where Gen X households had been in 2001. The gap was caused by lower earnings and higher education costs.

25 Why has college debt become such a problem?

The reason is skyrocketing costs, according to the College Board. It estimates four years of college tuition, room and board nearly tripled from $16,630 in 1981-1982 to $45,370 in 2016-2017. That is in 2016 dollars. The Institute for College Access and Success reported that more than two-thirds of 2015's seniors graduated with student loan debt.

Debt averaged $30,100, up 4 percent from 2014. In 2018, The Fed reported that student debt topped $1.5 trillion, up from $600 billion in 2008. The Fed has estimated that average monthly payments on student loans rose from $227 in 2005 to $393 in 2016. Student debt repayment is slower among people with lower incomes. Statistically, that includes more people who are Black and Hispanic, or who attended for-profit schools.

26 How are Millennials handling debt?

Unfortunately, they keep borrowing. Many turn to credit cards, which are easy to get but charge higher interest rates. Northwestern Mutual's 2018 Planning & Progress Study looked at 2,000 adults, with 600 Millennials among them. It found that Millennials between 25 and 34 had an average of $42,000 in debt. About a quarter of that was on credit cards. Sixteen percent was student loan debt.

27 Are Millennials buying homes?

They are, but they do it later than earlier generations. This may be connected to their older average marriage age as well as finances. In 2016, the Census Bureau said home ownership had fallen to 62.9 percent, tying the low of 1965 when it began tracking. The high was more than 69 percent in 2005. Millennials want to own homes—more than 90 percent said so in one study—but most feel they

cannot yet afford one. With 89 million potential home buyers, builders and banks hope for a Millennials home-buying binge. Apartment List put the question of home ownership to 6,400 Millennial renters and nearly half said they had nothing saved for a down payment.

28 Are they happy homeowners?

Almost two-thirds of Millennials reported some remorse, compared with 44 percent of home buyers overall in a 2019 survey by Bankrate.com. The top reason for Millennial regret was unexpected maintenance or hidden costs. Twenty-five percent reported this feeling.

29 What are Millennials' attitudes toward car ownership?

As a group, Millennials make these purchases at older ages than prior generations. According to the J.D. Power Information Network, Millennial new-car ownership spiked at 28 percent. Millennials also chose to get driver's licenses later. As a more urban demographic, they rely more on mass transit and sharing services such as Zipcar, Uber and Lyft.

30 Are Millennials poor?

A Census Bureau analysis showed the poverty rate for adults 18-34 was about 15 percent in 1980, 1990 and 2000. In 2009-2013, when Millennials were that

age, the rate hit 20 percent. Pew noted Millennials are a more diverse generation and that minorities in every generation have higher poverty rates.

31 What about the gender gap in pay?

Millennials are the largest generation in the workforce, and they have the highest proportion of women workers. The gap between men and women's pay is less than it has been for Gen X and Baby Boomers. But the picture could change as Millennials age. Gen Xers and Boomers found that women's pay fell behind when they started having children. At the top of the wage scale, the number of women CEOs in Fortune 500 companies declined by 25 percent from 2017 to 2018.

32 What are Millennials' spending habits?

Millennials have been mocked as the "cheapest generation." That could be interpreted as being frugal, broke or less interested in material goods. Millennials have been portrayed as having less interest in buying. But that might not be true, according to a 2018 study from the Federal Reserve. "We find little evidence that Millennial households have tastes and preference for consumption that are lower than those of earlier generations ..." It examined demographics, income, spending, debt and net worth.

Work

33 What are Millennials' career ambitions?

Almost three-fourths of Millennials surveyed by the Economic Innovation Group said they believe that risk-taking leads to rewards. Even so, they said they preferred the corporate-ladder track over entrepreneurship, 44 percent to 22 percent. The formula may lie somewhere in between. Millennials say they want advancement, mentoring and work-life balance. This blend is not entirely found in one path or the other.

34 Do Millennials want to be their own bosses?

Millennials who can afford to start businesses may do so, but they are in the minority. "The Missing Millennial Entrepreneurs," by the U.S. Small Business Administration, showed that fewer than 2 percent of Millennials were self-employed in 2014. Generation X reported 7.6 percent, and Boomers reported 8.3 percent. The report also said older generations had begun their startups at younger ages.

35 Are Millennials off to good career starts?

This illustrates intra-generational variance. The first Millennials, born in 1981, started their careers as the economy was sliding into the Great Recession. For those with college degrees, the unemployment rate was 8 percent. This made it hard to start and sustain careers. Late Millennials who started careers in 2018 walked into the lowest unemployment in 50 years and found far greater opportunity. In 2010, according to the U.S. Congress' Joint Economic Committee, the unemployment rate for 16- to 24-year-olds with only a high school diploma was 24.6 percent.

36 What are top career choices for Millennials?

While individual career choices depend heavily on desire, demand drives the job market. Millennials have a wide range of career interests. The U.S. Bureau of Labor Statistics projects healthcare to become the largest employer by 2024. That has more to do with the expected health needs of aging Boomers and Gen Xers than the interests of Millennials.

37 Is the job-hopping Millennial an accurate stereotype?

Early studies seemed to confirm this. They compared young, early-career people to older ones. However,

a 2017 Pew analysis of Department of Labor data contradicts this. Pew found Millennials "are just as likely to stick with their employers as their older counterparts in Generation X were when they were young adults." It reported that college-educated Millennials stay with their employers longer than Generation X workers did in 2000 when they were at the same age. Pew concluded that the stereotype does not stick.

38 Do Millennial workers slack off?

Although a 2014 Gallup poll shows Millennials are less engaged with their jobs than other generations, the difference is small. Almost 29 percent of Millennials reported high work engagement, compared to 32.3 percent for Gen X. In no generation do most workers report high job engagement.

39 Do Millennials care about company values?

A study by Cone Communications showed Millennials pay attention to company values and are looking for specific ones. Seventy-five percent of Millennials said they would take less pay to work for a more responsible company. Seventy-six percent said they would consider the social and environmental commitment of the company. Sixty-four percent said they would not work at a company that lacks social responsibility.

40 Do Millennials think promotions will just be handed to them?

A Gallup poll indicates 87 percent of Millennials crave professional development and opportunities. Those who do not see development might leave. Gallup also reports Millennials are the generation most likely to look for new opportunities.

41 Are Millennials hypersensitive to criticism?

Millennials look for regular feedback, a result of being part of a strongly connected society, Gallup found. Those who received regular feedback were twice as engaged in their jobs. But don't expect them to ask for feedback—only 15 percent of Millennials say they regularly request it.

42 What do Millennials want from bosses?

Millennials crave growth and coaches—as opposed to bosses—and don't like to waste time on small issues, writes Jeff Fromm. He is president of the consumer trends consultancy FutureCast. He is also co-author of "Marketing to Millennials" and "Millennials with Kids." He said they want balance and democracy in the workplace.

43 Are Millennial women getting hired?

This group is surpassing men. A 2019 Bloomberg analysis of Bureau of Labor Statistics data found that Millennial women accounted for almost half the gains in the prime-age labor force in the three prior years. Male employment in the same group lagged. Bloomberg cited several reasons. Those included more women going to college and delays in marriage or having children. An increase in single-parent households meant more women were starting families. Lower employment rates and lower wages for men put more pressure on women to work.

Politics

44 When will Millennials be the largest voting generation?

The 2016-2020 elections are a tipping point. In the 2016 election, for the first time in decades, fewer than half the voters were Baby Boomers and older generations. A Pew analysis of Census data showed that Millennials and Gen Xers cast slightly more than half of 137.5 million total votes. Millennials cast 34 million votes, Gen X had 35.7 million. The number of Millennial voters is projected to surpass Gen X in 2020. TargetSmart, which analyzes political data, reported that voting in the 18-29 age group was up 188 percent in 2018. That group included some post-Millennial voters.

45 Do Millennials vote?

Voting power grows not just as a generation reaches voting age, but as more of its members exercise that right. Typically, the older people are, the more likely they are to vote. Turnout for voters aged 18-29 in the 2018 mid-term election was 31 percent, according to The Center for Information and Research on Civic Learning and Engagement. That was up 21 percent

from the mid-terms in 2014. The center called 2018's turnout "the highest level of participation among youth in the past quarter century." A poll by NBC News/GenForward before the 2018 mid-term elections found 7 percent of 18- to 34-year-olds said voting is too basic to bother with. Twelve percent said they probably would not vote. Twenty-three percent said they did not know.

46 How do Millennials vote?

A poll by KQED News found that roughly 55 percent of Millennial voters in 2016 went for Hillary Clinton. Thirty-seven percent voted for Donald Trump, and 8 percent voted for third-party or independent candidates. Pew reported a generational voting gap. Baby Boomers and older voters lean right. Millennials and Gen X are increasingly liberal. Millennials are the most politically liberal voting generation and more likely to identify as Democrats. An NBC analysis of the 2018 election noted that Democrats won the youth vote by 35 percentage points, a significant shift from their 11-point edge in 2014. There was also a growing gender gap. Women, who preferred Democrats by 4 percentage points in 2014, gave them a 19-point margin in 2018.

47 Are Millennials getting elected?

They are now. In 2016, Millennials were the largest living generation, but one third were not yet of

voting age. Five Millennials were elected to the 435-seat U.S. House of Representatives that year. Bloomberg reported that Millennials would have to hold 97 seats to reflect their numbers in the over-25 population, the age group eligible to serve in the U.S. House. All generations were under-represented except Baby Boomers. While their fair-share number of seats would have been 148, they held 270. The 2019-2020 Congress began with 26 Millennials. Most were Democrats.

48 Are women part of this political change?

Some people called 2018 a political "Year of the Woman." The 104 women elected or re-elected in 2018 were a record, 22 percent more than the 84 who won two years earlier. Also in 2018, six women won U.S. Senate seats, joining 10 who were already in the Senate. Senators must be 30.

Women in politics during the Millennial age

Ever since the first Millennials were born in 1981, there have been a number of milestones for women:

1981 Sandra Day O'Connor becomes the first woman on the Supreme Court.

1982 The Equal Rights Amendment falls short of ratification.

1984 Geraldine Ferraro is the first woman nominated to be vice president on a major-party ticket.

1997 Madeleine Albright becomes the first female U.S. secretary of state.

2007 Nancy Pelosi becomes the first female speaker of the U.S. House.

2008 Alaska Gov. Sarah Palin becomes the first woman to run for vice president on the Republican ticket. Hillary Rodham Clinton loses the Democratic nomination for president to Barack Obama.

2016 Clinton wins the Democratic presidential nomination, becoming the first woman to lead a major-party ticket. She loses to Donald Trump.

2018 Congress has a record number of women elected or re-elected, with 104 female House members including the youngest ever, 29-year-old Millennial Alexandria Ocasio-Cortez.

2019 The 42 women joining the U.S. House win more than 60 percent of the seats that Democrats flipped in what some call the "Year of the Woman." Four of the newly elected women are Republicans.

49 Is there a generation gap in women's feelings about harassment?

Whether older or younger than 35, women agree strongly on harassment, according to a 2018 study of 2,511 U.S. women by media companies Vox and Morning Consult. Their responses showed strong similarities about the extent to which they experience sexual harassment and their views on its effects and consequences.

Lifestyles

50 Do Millennials depend on parents for survival?

Support, yes, but not necessarily survival. Part of this is because parents want to help out. According to a 2015 Clark University Poll of Parents of Emerging Adults, about 74 percent of Millennials were receiving financial assistance from parents. Much was because of college debt.

51 How attuned are Millennials to what is going on in the world?

Two-thirds of Millennials consume news regularly. Forty percent of those consumers said in an Associated Press survey that they check the news multiple times a day.

52 News media or social media?

Some of each. According to the American Press Institute, 88 percent of Millennials learn about news from Facebook, 36 percent from Pinterest, 33 percent from Twitter, 23 percent from Reddit and

21 percent from Tumblr. Percentages total to more than 100 percent because people use more than one platform. Millennials also interact with news in ways not possible on older platforms. Six in 10, for instance, say they regularly click "like" on articles, headlines or links. For this generation, social media is a combination of seeking information, making referrals and following friends.

53 How much do Millennials shop online?

Millennials are the first generation to grow up with online shopping. It began in 1994, when the first Millennials were 13. A 2016 study by UPS and ComScore found that Millennials made 54 percent of their purchases online.

54 What about online banking?

According to Business Insider, nearly three-quarters of Millennials with bank accounts visit a branch once a month or less. Mobile payments and apps have made banking more convenient than ever. Some banking analysts say this will mean fewer automatic teller machines and brick-and-mortar banks.

Values

55 What are Millennials' values?

The World Economic Forum analyzed responses from more than 26,000 Millennials worldwide in 2017. More than 1,600 were in the United States. It asked people to rank five things that were missing from their society and that would make them feel more free. One value was more than twice as important as the others for U.S. Millennials:

Equal access to opportunities for all 59.6%
The ability to live without fear 25.3%
The ability to live and work anywhere 23.9%
Job security 23.2%
The ability to change the law/constitution 19.3%

56 What do Millennials worry about?

That study, called the Global Shapers Survey, also asked about concerns. About two-thirds of U.S. Millennials said their top concern was income inequality and discrimination. The next two concerns were government accountability/corruption and climate change. The fourth concern, cited by 24.1 percent of U.S. respondents, was lack of

healthcare. Worldwide, climate change was the top concern for Millennials.

57 Are Millennials religious?

Millennials lead a nationwide decline in religious affiliation, according to the Pew Research Center. Its 2015 Religious Landscape report updated research from 2007. The numbers of people who were religiously affiliated or who said they believe in God declined. The age group with the steepest decline from 2007 to 2014 was Millennials. Michael Hout, a professor of sociology at New York University, wrote that many Millennials' parents are Baby Boomers who let their children think for themselves and find their own moral compasses. Lower affiliation is not just in religion. Millennials also express less trust in the labor market, government and marriage.

58 Are Millennials patriotic?

This might depend on your definition of patriotism. An American National Election Study concluded that patriotism is declining among generations. It stated that about 45 percent of Millennials view their American identity as important. Boomers were at 67 percent. In terms of military service, only 4 percent of Millennial men are veterans, compared to 47 percent of Silent men. In terms of Constitutional freedoms, Pew found that Millennials are more likely than previous generations to be OK with limits on speech offensive to minorities. Some have

Millennial Religious Landscape

Pew Research Center 2015 Religious Landscape Study. "Other Christian Groups" included Mormons, Orthodox Christians, Jehovah's Witnesses and other smaller Christian groups.

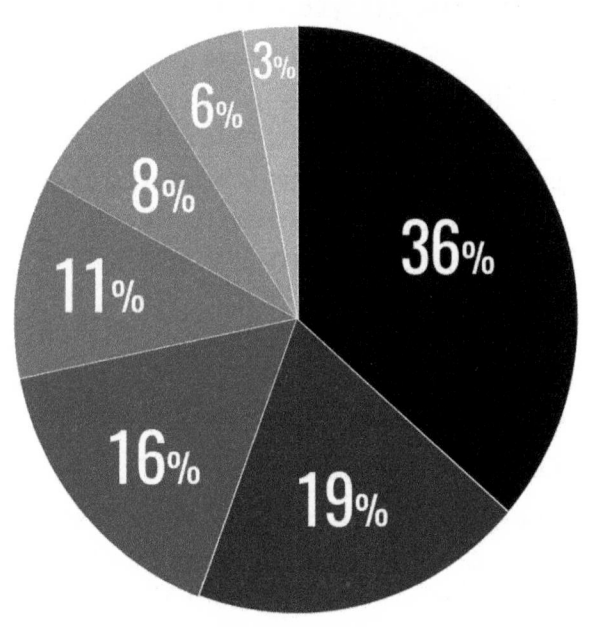

- Unaffiliated (36%)
- Evangelical Protestant (19%)
- Catholic (16%)
- Mainline Protestant (11%)
- Other Groups (8%)
- Historically Black Protestant (6%)
- Other Christian Groups (3%)

Graphic by Camille Douglas

said Millennials are more likely to favor stricter gun control, but surveys by Pew and Gallup dispute that.

59 What motivates Millennials?

The International Youth Foundation and YouGov found that Millennials want trust and respect. A Pew study found they are more likely to rank having a job they enjoy as extremely important. And another Pew study said Millennial priorities are being a good parent, having a successful marriage and helping others.

60 Do Millennials chafe under authority?

No, but they question it. In Forbes, Intern Sushi CEO Shara Senderoff said Millennials are more likely to question authority. The article said Millennials are products of Baby Boomer parents who spent their formative adult years questioning authority. Jamie Gutfreund of the Intelligence Group said Millennial workers do not like a "command and control" climate. They respond better to inclusive management.

Families

61 Do Millennials live at home longer?

According to a 2016 Pew report, for the first time in more than 130 years, it was more common for young adults to be living with parents than with a spouse or partner. This was especially true of men. Twenty-five percent of people aged 25-29 lived with a parent, up from 18 percent a decade earlier. For people aged 30-34, living with a parent rose from 9 percent to 13 percent. The Washington Post reported, "behind the trend are older Millennials, particularly those without college degrees, who are living at home." Why? The Great Recession and older generations staying in the labor force longer made it more difficult for some Millennials to get higher-paying jobs.

62 Are there other causes?

Apartment search firm Adobo blames the costs of rent and home ownership. It listed these metropolitan areas as having the largest percentages of Millennials still living at home:

Miami/Fort Lauderdale/West Palm Beach	44.8%
Riverside/San Bernardino/Ontario	44.5%
New York/Newark/Jersey City	43.8%
Los Angeles/Long Beach/Anaheim	41.5%
Philadelphia/Camden/Wilmington	41.0%
Detroit/Warren/Dearborn	40.0%

63 Are Millennials marrying later?

By 2014, 59 percent of Millennials had never been married. They also expected to wait longer to marry than previous generations had. This is according to Gallup's "Millennials, Marriage and Family."

64 Are there also fewer Millennials marrying?

Yes, according to Pew. Its "Survey on Millennials in Adulthood: Detached from Institutions, Networked with Friends" compared generations at the same age. It found that 26 percent of Millennials married versus 36 percent of Generation X and 48 percent of Baby Boomers. The Silent Generation was 65 percent.

65 What is the reason for later and fewer marriages?

The National Marriage Project's report, "Knot Yet" gave several reasons. Most were financial. A harsh job market and high college costs made many Millennials feel less confident than earlier generations about getting married.

66 Does this mean the number of unmarried parents is rising?

Yes, especially among Millennials with less education and income. A Johns Hopkins University study reported in 2016, "It is now unusual for non-college-graduates who have children in their teens and twenties to have all of them within marriage." Gallup found that unmarried parents are also more accepted.

67 Are Millennials also delaying childbirth?

The average age of first-time mothers in the United States in 2016 was 26.3, the highest in 45 years. The average age could continue to climb in the United States. In some countries, it is around 30. Contributing to the rising age of motherhood was a steep decline in the number of teen mothers, according to the National Center for Health Statistics.

68 How do Millennial parents raise their children?

A 2015 study by Time and Survey Monkey asked some unusual questions to get a different picture of this. Of 2,000 parents with children under 18, 81 percent had shared pictures of their kids on social media. Sixty percent said it was important for children to have unique names. Thirty percent expressed concern about other parents judging them for what they fed their children.

69 Do Millennials support same-sex marriage?

Seventy-one percent of Millennials supported same-sex marriage in 2016, according to Pew. That poll and others show that support for same-sex marriage has steadily increased from generation to generation.

Love and Sex

70 Are Millennials the "hookup" generation?

There is disagreement. Millennials are actually "not more promiscuous than their predecessors," according to Ryne Sherman, Ph.D. A study he co-authored found that of people between 20 and 24 years and born in the 1990s, 15 percent had no sexual partners since turning 18. That compared with 6 percent in the 1960s group. This generation is also twice as likely as Gen Xers were at the same age to be virgins. This comes from a study by San Diego State University professor Jean Twenge. On the other hand, a study published by the American Psychological Association said casual sex was becoming "increasingly normative among adolescents and young adults in North America ..."

71 Are Millennials involved in more "open relationships?"

The theory is that avoiding monogamous relationships has led to more in which partners agree they may have sex with other people. In contrast, several studies show that Millennials are having less sex than Gen X did.

72 How significant is online dating?

According to Pew, online dating had its greatest increase from 2013 to 2015 among younger and older adults. For adults 18-24, it nearly tripled from 10 to 27 percent. For adults aged 55-64, the increase was from 6 to 12 percent. Across most age groups, about a third of people say they know someone who formed a long-term relationship through online dating.

73 Do Millennials divorce more?

Just the opposite. Millennials and Gen Xers have brought down the national divorce rate by 18 percent. A 2018 University of Maryland study showed this decrease from 2008 to 2016. One reason is that younger generations have been moving into marriage more slowly than older generations, which have higher rates of divorce. For example, the divorce rate for Boomers tripled between 1990 and 2015, according to the National Center for Family and Marriage Research.

Health

74 What peculiar health issues do Millennials face?

Millennial magazine cited four. They are celiac disease, dental issues, mental health and lack of health insurance. The insurance has a lot to do with moving off parents' plans and whether early employers provide insurance.

75 Are Millennials more stressed out than others?

The American Psychological Association has reported that 12 percent of Millennials have been diagnosed with an anxiety disorder. Nineteen percent have been diagnosed with depression. Both rates are higher than for older generations. Millennials and Gen Xers are also stressed about being stressed out. Sixty-two percent of Millennials and 63 percent of Gen Xers said they had tried to reduce their stress in the prior five years. That was slightly more than the 59 percent of Boomers. Even so, one fourth of Millennials and Gen Xers said they were not doing enough to combat stress. That compared to 15 percent of Boomers.

76 Are Millennials more medicated?

Express Scripts noted that the number of young adults medicated for ADHD soared from 2008 to 2012, particularly among young women. Use was up 85 percent. The percentage of people on antidepressants almost doubled from 6.9 percent in 1999 to 13 percent in 2012, according to the Journal of the American Medical Association.

77 Do Millennials use more recreational drugs?

Although social media might make it seem so, studies show just the opposite. According to DrugAbuse, the most commonly used substance for all four generations was alcohol, with a peak of 80 percent. Marijuana use was higher by Boomers, at 50 percent, than among Gen Xers and Millennials at 30-35 percent. Boomers used sedatives three times more than both Gen Xers and Millennials, and abused cocaine twice as much as Gen Xers and Millennials. Millennials led in the use of painkillers. More than 12 percent of people aged 19-20 reported recent painkiller abuse, compared to 8 percent of Gen Xers and Boomers.

78 How common is suicide among Millennials?

Suicide has become more common among each successive generation. In 2018, the U.S. Centers for Disease Control and Prevention reported that suicide is a leading cause of death in the United States. Rates increased in nearly every state from 1999 through 2016. According to the agency, "suicide is the third leading cause of death among persons aged 10-14 and the second among persons aged 15-34." Those were largely Millennials. For people aged 35-44, suicide was the fourth leading cause. It was fifth among people aged 45-54 years and eighth among people 55-64.

79 Are Millennials more prone to allergies?

According to the Asthma and Allergy Foundation of America, allergies are increasing. It reports that nasal allergies affect about 50 million people in the United States. The rate is 30 percent of adults and 40 percent among children. Asthma and other allergic diseases are the fifth leading chronic disease in the United States. They are the third most prevalent chronic disease for children under 18.

80 Do Millennials work out?

Eighty-eight percent of Millennials exercise regularly. However according to Small Biz Daily, Millennials

are not much healthier than their parents. They tend to enjoy forms of exercise beyond the traditional gym membership. This may include going for a hike or run, yoga or joining a fitness club with friends. For Millennials, working out is as much of an experience as it is about health.

81 What is the obesity rate for Millennials?

Millennials had a lower obesity rate than older generations in a Gallup-Healthways Well Being Index report in 2016. This bucked the trend of younger generations being more obese than prior ones. Comparative youth and its metabolism may be on Millennials' side, however. The report warned that Millennials do not eat as well as older generations and that they drink and smoke more.

82 Are Millennials turning to vegetarianism?

According to The New York Times, about 12 percent of Millennials classify themselves as "faithful vegetarians." That compares to 4 percent of Generation X and 1 percent of Baby Boomers. According to The Washington Post and QSR Magazine, Millennials have less money than older generations but spend their money in ways they feel make a difference. That includes food choices.

83 Are Millennials obsessed with appearance?

University of Georgia psychology professor W. Keith Campbell has written three books on generational narcissism. He wrote that Millennials are bombarded with narcissistic images on television and in the media and that they have adopted those traits. Millennials raised by "Me Generation" Boomers were taught to curate self-image. This is compounded by smartphone cameras and the importance of seeking peer validation through photo sharing.

Culture

84 Are Millennials called that in other countries?

Although this guide focuses on the United States, generations span the globe, especially when they share experiences in culture, economics, technology, politics and conflict. Many countries worldwide consider this to be a distinct generation. It is referred to in different ways. Some are direct translations of Millennials or Generation Y. Some names are unique to their countries.

85 Are Millennials more connected to society than earlier generations?

Two Pew studies give us an idea. One found that Millennials are less attached to traditional political and religious institutions. Instead, they relate to networks of friends, co-workers and others through social media. The other said Millennials in the United States and around the world have a far more expansive view of what it means for people to be "one of us."

86 How are Millennials changing the language?

According to The Washington Post, linguists call the Millennial shortening of words to "effect a certain tone" as "totesing." Examples are "actch" for actually and "bill" for billion. Word abbrevs are used in texting and creep into spoken language. Some criticize totes as unprofesh.

87 What is some Millennial slang?

Slang, by nature, is in-group, not universal and transitory. It can sound inauthentic when used by others. Slang changes so quickly that by the time outsiders catch on, it has changed. Millennials, like every generation, have their own slang. Much is local or regional. And some Millennials use slang ironically or as parodies. Millennial slang has sprung from celebrities, social media sites including Twitter and Vine (remember that?) and texting.

Here is some:

bae Before Anyone Else; the most significant other.

curve To dodge an obvious expression of interest: "I was trying to catch this girl's eye, but she curved."

dank Cool.

extra Over the top, dramatic.

fomo Fear of Missing Out, often caused by seeing posts about others' dank lives.

on fleek Fashionable, on point, perfect. "Your hair is on fleek."

receipts Evidence, often in texts or social media, that someone is being hypocritical.

throwing shade Making subtle negative comments about someone.

troll Trying to provoke someone.

88 Did Millennials change the pound sign to the hashtag?

In 2014, the Oxford English Dictionary added hashtag as a name for #. Officially, it is called an octothorpe for its eight points. The OED speculated that hashtag grew out of "hatch mark," and that "hash" was being used in the computer and telecommunication fields in 1961. The symbol has also been called "the number sign" and some journalists used to end their typed copy with ###. One #oldschool Boomer professor calls the hashtag "the Tic-Tac-Toe sign."

89 Did Millennials popularize emojis?

Emoji is Japanese for picture-character. The little social media pictures were first used on Japanese phones in the 1990s. Millennials grew up with them. Unicode standardizes emoji across platforms and catalogues them on emojipedia.org. Categories include Animals and Nature, Food and Drink, and Smileys & People, who now come in different skin tones. There are thousands. According to emojipedia.

org, the most popular ones are a person shrugging, a face with tears of joy, a red heart, and a smiley face with heart eyes. Emoji and emoticon are similar words, but mean different things. Emoticons are made by typing characters that make a picture. This one means sleeping: (-_-)zzz. Some emoticons, such as the smiley face, became early emojis. They became more elaborate and, in 2018, Unicode introduced superheroes and supervillains, a llama, skateboard and moon cake. One study said emojis make up 40 percent of social messaging. A 2015 Adobe study said Millennials are comfortable using emojis to communicate with supervisors and top bosses. Companies, celebrities and politicians, including Hillary Clinton, have custom emojis. These are drafts from emojipedia.org of symbols planned for 2019:

Source: https://emojipedia.org/emojipedia/12.0/new/

90 Are there Millennial hipsters?

A New York Times article said hipsters wear "skinny jeans and big eyeglasses, gather in tiny enclaves in big cities, and look down on mainstream fashions and 'tourists.'" There are subgroups of hipsters based on profession and class. They are in several generations. One more thing: Most hipsters do not call themselves hipsters, just as most Millennials do not like to be called Millennials. Only 40 percent of Millennials consider themselves to be that.

Entertainment

91 What do Millennials watch?

This has as much to do with devices as it does with content. Technology has shattered the idea of people gathering at the same time or place to watch TV. Thirty-four percent of Millennials watch more video online than on TV, according to a New York Times survey. It found that 44 percent of Millennials who favor online video said cellphones let them watch what they like, whenever they wish. The percentage of this generation that even owns a TV is lower than it is for others. Millennials lead the tide toward online streaming services such as Netflix or Hulu with instant access, customized experiences and variety.

92 Which leaders do Millennials admire?

The World Economic Forum polled 1,000 Millennials from 125 countries and 285 cities. Among leaders, Nelson Mandela was mentioned most often. The list continued with Pope Francis, Elon Musk, Mahatma Gandhi, Bill Gates, Barack Obama, Richard Branson, Steve Jobs, Mohammad Yunus, Narendra Modi and Warren Buffett.

Education

93 What is the average educational level for Millennials?

According to the Census Bureau, 86.7 percent of Millennials had at least a high school diploma in 2012-2015. Pew estimates that Millennials' education levels will surpass those of Gen Xers and Boomers.

94 How are Millennials changing college?

A big change is in who is going to college. Now, more women than men earn college degrees. This is a flip from the Silent Generation, according to Pew. Among Millennials aged 21-36 in 2017, women with bachelor's degrees outnumbered men with them, 36 percent to 29 percent. Gen Xers were the first generation of women to outpace men in degrees, with a 3-percentage-point advantage.

Millennials are the Most Educated Generation to Date

Percent (%) completing at least a bachelor's degree at ages 18-33

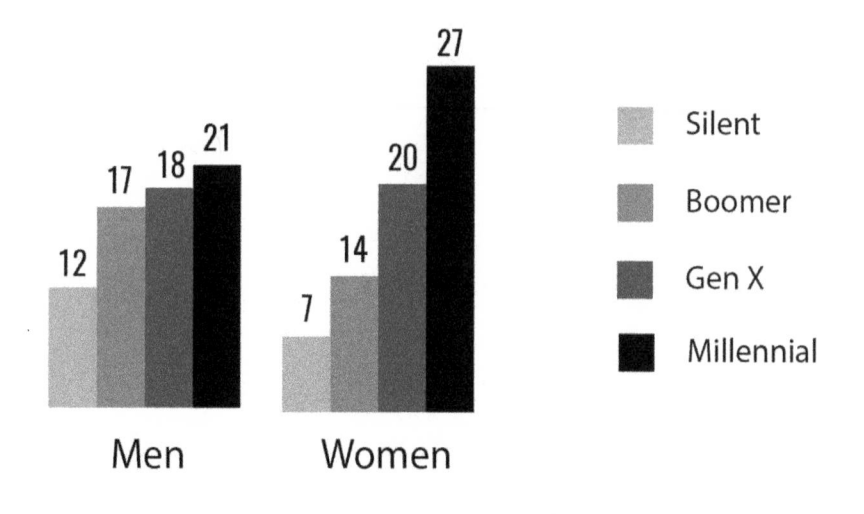

Men

Women

Silent

Boomer

Gen X

Millennial

Source: Pew Research Center (2015)

Graphic by Camille Douglas

95 What proportion of Millennials graduate from college?

According to the U.S. Census Bureau, 57.3 percent of Millennials in 2012 had some college. Thirty-one percent graduated with a bachelor's degree. More than 8 percent had master's degrees, and 3.1 percent had doctoral or professional degrees.

96 How do U.S. Millennials stack up academically in the world?

U.S. Millennials are weaker in literacy, numeracy and problem solving in technology-rich environments. This comes from a 2015 study by the Educational Testing Service. It raised questions about Millennials' potential for higher-level jobs and U.S. competitiveness with other countries.

97 What are the most common majors for Millennials?

U.S. News & World Report compared Boomers' choices in 1970 to Millennials' choices 40 years later. It showed business degrees were up strongly and education majors were down from 21 percent of all degrees to 6 percent. Social and behavioral sciences were down from 11.5 percent to about 6 percent. All other majors remained pretty even but below 5 percent throughout the period.

Impact

98 What are Millennials' priorities?

Millennials want what older generations have said they want. Pew reported that family outweighed fame and fortune. The top priorities, in order, were being a good parent, having a good marriage, helping others, owning a home, living a very religious life, being successful in a high-paying career and lots of free time. Millennials' top worries, according to a narrower survey by Country Financial, are about retirement and healthcare expenses.

99 Do Millennials volunteer?

Millennials are more involved in volunteering and service than older generations, according to a Pew report based on a panel of experts. Pew reported Millennials are using technology to revitalize activism and community action.

100 Who are some well-known Millennials?

Millennials include Facebook creator **Mark Zuckerburg** and women and children's activist and youngest-ever Nobel Prize laureate **Malala Yousafzai** of Pakistan.

Some celebrity Millennials:

Acting: **Aziz Ansari, Nicholas Hoult, Michael B. Jordan, Anna Kendrick, Zoë Kravitz, Jennifer Lawrence, Lupita Nyong'o, Eddie Redmayne, Emma Stone, Constance Wu**

Comedy: **Amy Schumer**

Design: **Nicole Richie**

Music: **Adele, Beyoncé, Justin Bieber, Ciara, Lady Gaga, Selena Gomez, Bruno Mars, Rihanna, Taylor Swift, Justin Timberlake**

Rap: **Chance the Rapper, Drake, Yo Gotti, Nicki Minaj**

Sports: **Usain Bolt**, track; **Carli Lloyd**, soccer; **Danica Patrick**, driving; **Roger Federer, Serena** and **Venus Williams**, tennis

Resources

Books

Deal, Jennifer J. and Alec Levenson. What Millennials Want from Work: How to Maximize Engagement in Today's Workforce. New York: McGraw-Hill Education. 2016.

Espinoza, Chip. Managing the Millennials: Discover the Core Competencies for Managing Today's Workforce, edition 2, Hoboken: Wiley. 2016.

Gordinier, Jeff. X Saves the World: How Generation X Got the Shaft but Can Still Keep Everything from Sucking. New York: Penguin reprint. 2009.

Harris, Malcolm. Kids These Days: Human Capital and the Making of Millennials. Boston: Little, Brown and Company. 2017.

Howe, Neil. Millennials Rising: The Next Great Generation. New York: Vintage Books. 2000.

Howe, Neil and William Strauss. Generations: The History of America's Future, 1584 to 2069. New York: William Morrow & Company, 1991.

Jenkins, Ryan. The Millennial Manual: The Complete How-To Guide to Manage, Develop, and Engage Millennials at Work. Independently published. 2017.

Johnson, Meagan and Larry Johnson. Generations, Inc.: From Boomers to Linksters–Managing the Friction Between Generations at Work. New York: Amacom. 2010.

Mulrennan, Mia. Passed Over and Pissed Off: The Overlooked Leadership Talents of Generation X. Minneapolis: Rave-Worthy LLC. 2015.

Rushkoff, Douglas. GenX Reader. New York: Ballantine Books. 1993.

Shaw, Haydn. Sticking Points: How to Get 4 Generations Working Together in the 12 Places They Come Apart. Carole Stream: Tyndale House Publishers. 2013.

Smith, Tim. Dare Mighty Things: A Field Guide for Millennial Entrepreneurs. Campbell: FastPencil Publishing. 2017.

Strauss, Williams and Neil Howe. 13th Gen: Abort, Retry, Ignore, Fail? New York: Vintage, 1993.

Taylor, Paul. The Next America: Boomers, Millennials, and the Looming Generational Showdown. New York: PublicAffairs. 2016.

Tulgan, Bruce. Not Everyone Gets a Trophy: How to Manage the Millennials. New York: Jossey-Bass. 2016.

Twenge, Jean M. Generation Me—Revised and Updated: Why Today's Young Americans Are More Confident, Assertive, Entitled—and More Miserable than Ever Before. New York: Atria Books, 2014.

Twenge, Jean M. iGen: Why Today's Super-Connected Kids Are Growing Up Less Rebellious, More Tolerant, Less Happy—and Completely Unprepared for Adulthood—and What That Means for the Rest of Us. New York: Atria Books. 2017

Zemke, Ron. Generations at Work: Managing the Clash of Boomers, Gen Xers, and Gen Yers in the Workplace. New York: Amacom. 2013.

Reports

Achieve. The Millennial Impact Project. 2017. http://www.themillennialimpact.com/about/

The Brookings Institution, William H. Frey: The Millennial Generation: A Demographic Bridge to America's Diverse Future. 2018. https://www.brookings.edu/research/millennials/

CAF America. Generation G: The Millennials and How They Are Changing the Art of Giving. 2015. http://www.cafamerica.org/generation-g-the-Millennials-and-how-they-are-changing-the-art-of-giving/

Deloitte. The Millennial Survey: Millennials' Confidence in Business, Loyalty to Employers Deteriorate. 2018. deloitte.com/millennialsurvey

Development Dimensions International DDI, The Conference Board and EY. Global Leadership Forecast 2018. https://www.ddiworld.com/glf2018

Federal Reserve Bank of St. Louis. A Lost Generation? Long-Lasting Wealth Impacts of the Great Recession on Young Families. 2018. https://www.stlouisfed.org/~/media/files/pdfs/hfs/essays/hfs_essay_2_2018.pdf?la=en

Federal Reserve Board Divisions of Research & Statistics and Monetary Affairs Discussion Series. Are Millennials Different? 2018. https://www.federalreserve.gov/econres/feds/files/2018080pap.pdf

Gallup. Millennials, Marriage and Family. 2015. https://news.gallup.com/poll/191462/gallup-analysis-millennials-marriage-family.aspx

National Association of Realtors. Home Buyer and Seller Generational Trends Report. 2017. https://www.

nar.realtor/sites/default/files/reports/2017/2017-home-buyer-and-seller-generational-trends-03-07-2017.pdf

Pew Research Center. 40% of Millennials OK with Limiting Speech Offensive to Minorities. 2015. http://www.pewresearch.org/fact-tank/2015/11/20/40-of-millennials-ok-with-limiting-speech-offensive-to-minorities/

Pew Research Center. The Generation Gap in American Politics. 2018. http://www.people-press.org/2018/03/01/the-generation-gap-in-american-politics/

Pew Research Center. Index to reports. http://www.pewresearch.org/topics/millennials/

Pew Research Center. Millennials: A Portrait of Generation Next: Confident. Connected. Open to Change. 2010. http://www.pewresearch.org/wp-content/uploads/sites/3/2010/10/millennials-confident-connected-open-to-change.pdf

Pew Research Center. Millennials Aren't Job-Hopping Any Faster than Generation X Did. 2017. http://www.pewresearch.org/fact-tank/2017/04/19/millennials-arent-job-hopping-any-faster-than-generation-x-did/

Stanford Center on Longevity. The Milestones Project. 2018. http://longevity.stanford.edu/2018/02/06/milestones/

Transamerica Center for Retirement Studies. Perspectives on Retirement: Baby Boomers, Generation X, and Millennials. 2016. https://www.transamericacenter.org/docs/default-source/retirement-survey-of-workers/tcrs2016_sr_perspectives_on_retirement_baby_boomers_genx_Millennials.pdf

University of Michigan. The Generation X Report. 2012. http://lsay.org/GenX_2012Vol2Iss1.pdf

White House Council of Economic Advisers: 15 Economic Facts About Millennials. 2014. https://obamawhitehouse.archives.gov/sites/default/files/docs/millennials_report.pdf

World Economic Forum. Shapers Survey. 2017. http://shaperssurvey2017.org/static/data/WEF_GSC_Annual_Survey_2017.pdf